HANDS ON MINDFULNESS

HOW TO USE CREATIVE HANDWORK TO HELP YOU THROUGH CHALLENGING TIMES.

LAUREN KINGSLAND

For more information, email books@laurenkingsland.com

ISBN: 978-0-9787044-9-0 - Paperback

IS78-0-9787044-3-8 - eBook

DEDICATION

To my parents whose busy hands taught and inspired me to a richer life.

Ruthie Lindal Swain, *my teacher, who started my hands-on making journey when I was 5 with an embroidery needle and floss to stitch letters on Daddy's handkerchief.*

Pervis A. Swain, *my role model, whose capable hands were always busy - carving wooden birds, folding paper stars, tying flies, or improvising a gadget to make a job easier.*

To my sister, Carla Swain Bonifasi, *who loves making things as much as I do and is always only a phone call away.*

To Claire Wagner, *aka "The Knitter", who was a beloved artist-in-residence with the Georgetown Lombardi Arts & Humanities Program for over 15 years. She inspired scores of knitters, fostered a creative community, and was our role model for being an engaged, creative elder well into her nineties.*

ACKNOWLEDGMENTS

Special thanks to Chappell Kingsland and Carla Bonifasi, for being supportive witnesses to the process of writing and for their faith that things will work out as they should.

Thanks to Ben Allen-Kingsland, Deborah Bardsley, Janet Beavin, Michelle Berberet, Carrie Monger, and Susan Moser for early reading and feedback..

Thanks to Julia Langley, Director of the Georgetown Lombardi Arts and Humanities Program and my colleague artists-in-residence for being a community in service of creative change for better health.

Thanks also to -

Editor Extraordinaire Sandra Wissinger for her expertise and enthusiasm about the project.

Coach Brett Hilker at Selfpublishing.com for his guidance and holding me accountable.

Massage experts Mary Kathleen Rose, for Comfort Touch® massage training materials, and Jane Walton for her introduction to the Comfort Touch® methods.

TABLE OF CONTENTS

INTRODUCTION

This book is for anyone who has ever had a rough day and turned to their craft supply stash for a mental health break. It is for the person who is uncomfortable with idle hands. It is for someone facing the scary times of not knowing what is ahead. It is about creative coping. For example, a bed-ridden patient and the caregiver sitting beside them can both benefit physically and mentally from the perspective shift of hands-on mindfulness. To be clear, the concepts in this book will not magically fix anything, any more than the mere presence of a kitchen guarantees the appearance of dinner. These ideas are tools that can be applied to shift from feeling stuck in a bad rut to feeling like there is a way out. All challenges of life, large and small, are the lessons through which we grow, mature and gain compassion for one another. I offer here some direct, practical tools to help with mastery of those lessons.

Full disclosure: It is in my nature to make things, and I particularly love working with fibers. As a child I embroidered letters on Daddy's linen handkerchiefs. My troll dolls had elaborate felt outfits, complete with hats. I threaded needles for one grandmother when she made matching comforters for the bedroom I shared with my sister, Carla. Our other grandmother taught me to crochet. I learned to knit and tat from family friends. As a teenager I made all my clothes. I tried my hand at whatever creative medium came along—drawing, painting, ceramics, fly-tying, screen printing, dollmaking, needlepoint, cross-stitch, crewel, and weaving. I learned every way I could. Sometimes I took a class. Sometimes a friend showed me how. Often learning came with the help of a book, by bashing along to figure it out by myself.

"Study hard what interests you the most in the most undisciplined, irreverent, and original manner possible."—Richard Feynman

"One learns from books and by example only that certain things can be done. Actual learning requires that you do those things."—Frank Herbert

At age 15, injuries from a bicycling accident kept me laid up for several frustrating months. The much-needed lesson of patience came to me by stitching to pass the time. Instead of fretting about what I could not do, I became involved in what I could do. I made yo-yos into clown dolls and did cross-stitch. Having a handwork project in progress became a lifelong habit from then on. This personal experience of the power of handwork during convalescence was to inform my career.

In college I studied ancient Greek, the humanities, music, mathematics and computer science. My first job was designing craft projects for the Recreation Therapy department at the Clinical Center at National Institutes of Health in Bethesda, MD. That launched a career using hands-on projects to serve the community at NIH and later also at the Medstar Georgetown Lombardi Comprehensive Cancer Center through the fledgling Arts & Humanities Program. The lessons from these early years of making something in the presence of a medical situation became a valuable resource for this work.

Handwork can be the reason to focus on a topic other than illness. When a clinic patient began to work with me on a quilt kit or a beaded bracelet their posture would change. They would relax and focus and open up. They'd chat, ask questions or share experiences. People enjoy talking about their own lives and interests. I'd hear about treasured heirloom quilts that were reminders of loved ones and good times. The focus on making things created a bond that led to conversation. Patients were happier, distracted from their pain, and taken out of difficulty for a little while. Human connection is powerful medicine. And the products of hands can represent that connection. Through trial and error I learned 1) Keep the activity simple, and 2) Listen.

As we use our hands creatively, a positive shift happens. This shift away from struggle to a place of focus and creative action is repeatable. It is part of who we are; our bodies and our minds always affect one another, because both are essential, interwoven parts of human beings. A change in the mind can influence a change in our body and vice versa. It works both ways.

In this book we will look at ways to tap into this Mind-Body Connection by using the tools of active hands in service of more awareness and cooperation between the mind and body. My years of experience and observation lie behind these ideas and exercises. Begin with yourself, and then you can assist others to access their own internal connection.

The goal of this book is to promote a balanced whole self in the presence of both normal life and unusual challenges. The goal is to create a space for self-examination while your hands are busy in order for you to embrace the unique and wonderful you. You are probably already doing this in your own way, perhaps without even acknowledging it to yourself.

Scientific research is on-going about the effects of various physical actions on health and well being. Results are confirming what we intuitively know; the body influences the mind, and the mind influences the body. When we are upset we take a walk. When we are nervous we wring our hands together. We fidget or move to calm ourselves during anxiety. To give ourselves courage, we pause and take a deep breath. When our body is injured or unwell it affects our mood. It is my hope that together we can deliberately tap into this integration so we can all be happier, more resilient, and healthier.

This book is especially for makers—those who like to express their creativity through the process of transforming simple physical objects (materials) into things that are complex, useful, decorative, or beautiful. It is also for caregivers, parents, and anyone going through any kind of transition. Through this book, I want to give everyone permission to say boldly, "My therapy is (quilting, knitting, or other handwork of choice)."

There are many paths to tapping into the Mind-Body Connection. Some people meditate, do yoga, hike/exercise, make music, etc. If focusing on the movement of hands to make something is not your preferred way of reaching a peaceful, balanced state, that's fine. I challenge you to pay attention to your own behavior in this realm. This book presents tools that may serve you, or not. As you read, allow yourself to be inspired to use your own gifts, talents and skills in a deeper, more intentional way to bring you to a peaceful state.

Healing happens within us. When something goes out of balance or is injured our bodies work hard to restore themselves to health and wholeness. For more serious dis-ease we seek outside help to speed up this process. Remedies may range from chicken soup and ginger tea to over the counter products to prescription medications to chemotherapy. We seek relief ranging from a wet cloth on the forehead, a band-aid, a massage, a chiropractor or acupuncture, to setting a bone, surgery, infusions or radiation. All these remedies and treatments are our efforts to influence the healing process, to change the conditions in which our body's own healing process can work. Our mental health and our emotional self also need tending as our bodies heal or are restored to wholeness. And healing takes time. Finding a creative and therapeutic way to use your hands during a time of illness and convalescence reduces anxiety and stress to allow access to a calmer mind to support physical healing.

CHAPTER 1

THE HANDS WANT TO EXPRESS THEMSELVES

This chapter sets the stage for using your hands in ways that lead you to a happier life.

Today you may be unsure and unsettled. We all struggle to manage the hectic pace of life and change in today's world. Our phones and emails bombard us with notifications. We are busy, with places to go, things that need to be done, and expectations to be met, real or perceived. Our challenges are personal; each of us struggles in our own way. Stresses may come from work, family and other relationships, finances, physical or mental health issues, or something more uniquely our own. Personally, we have a lot to face.

The world's complex, interrelated, and serious global concerns swirl around us - we hear about the climate, economy, wars, politics, diseases—the list goes on. Stories of terrible things seem to surface all the time, evoking emotional responses and feelings of outrage. We cannot do anything about many of these problems. It is understandable that we feel helplessness, mental paralysis and frustration.

The combination of personal and broader concerns compounds our feeling of being overwhelmed and unsettled. These external pressures also affect our physical self that in turn influence our health and sense of well-being. We may feel what some experts term "dis-ease", a sense of not being at ease. The stresses in your life may indeed be making you sick. We long for a simple cure-all that fixes everything.[1]

An answer has been here the whole time, on hand so to speak. The secret? When we focus on activity with our hands we can help integrate and achieve a fresh perspective on life. This book is a set of tools to help you create space in your day, and in your mind to respond positively to whatever you face. It contains a series of true stories and suggestions for tapping into our existing human mind-body wisdom by **taking time to use our hands in a creative and mindful way.** A racing mind will slow down as you move. You will learn to reach an oasis of Flow State in which you don't have to think for a while about the noise and crush of modern concerns. Your body will respond in positive ways: lower heart rate and blood pressure, deeper breathing, calmer mental processes, perhaps a reduction of pain, or an understanding of the transient nature of upset and discomfort.

Remember, human history is long and stretches through many cultures around the world. You are unique here today AND millions have lived before us and our descendants will follow when we have passed. We humans have been given many gifts; one of the most special is the opposable thumb which lets us touch, grasp, and shape the world around us. Our nature is to invent, be curious and experiment. We express our inner lives through creativity - by making things, both useful and beautiful. We love telling jokes and stories, writing poetry, making music, singing and dancing. We humans are resilient, resourceful, adaptable and above all creative. This is to remind you to celebrate the best parts of humanity: creativity and the joy that it inspires. That joy is really the theme of this book.

The Mind-Body Connection is Yours Already. The concepts of holistic health and wellness, mindfulness, meditation or the Mind-Body Connection show up in magazines, news articles,

---

[1] By Phylameana lila Desy. Updated on May 08, 2019.

Phylameana lila Desy, the author of "The Everything Guide to Reiki," is a freelance writer, holistic healing consultant, intuitive counselor, and an energy medicine practitioner.

The word disease comes from old French, then to Middle English, and means "lack of ease." So the choice by members of the alternative medicine community to hyphenate the word is not as unusual as it first seems.

Individuals and professionals within the alternative healing community choose to hyphenate the word disease in order to reduce the emphasis on the pathology itself and to bring the focus instead to the natural state of ease that they wish to achieve through their therapies and outlook.

newsletters and blogs every day. Many voices urge us to slow down and be more in the moment by doing simple activities that bring us joy. Medical journals report on new clinical research exploring the impact of creativity and exposure to the Arts. So what are we actually talking about? My life as a maker, a handwork teacher and an artist in healthcare settings has taught me some insights that I will share with you to help you live more fully with whatever is happening in and around you.

Mind-Body Connection is the natural balance between our physical and mental selves. The world of computer and phone screens pushes us to live in our heads. An interconnected world of devices bombards us with so much information, we become confused, hurried, harried. Self-doubt, depression, and related physical manifestations creep in. We crave a return to a core of peacefulness that we believe, or hope, is at the center of our true self. But, wait!! We are NOT just disembodied heads. The good news is that, even if we aren't paying attention, our Mind-Body Connection is already in place. To use a technical metaphor, it is part of our original equipment. We do not need to enable it, or upgrade it to make it work. Being more aware of how our physical and mental sides are connected can help us appreciate our embodied selves and gain a deeper appreciation of our amazing multifaceted wholes.

Try this exercise: Smile a big grin. Pay attention to shifts in your posture, your eyes, and the rest of your body. Notice shifts in your emotions and thoughts as you smile. Do memories of things or people pop up? You have just accessed the back and forth nature of Mind-Body Connection.

Small physical changes can have a big influence on your mental and emotional state. The mental-physical cooperation system is constantly readjusting as things change, not unlike the shifts in center of gravity we make when riding a bike. In the face of anxiety, worry or whatever has separated you from awareness of your body, this book will help you be in touch with yourself—your whole self.

Life challenges large and small will still happen. The techniques in this book will not "fix" anything; they will help you gain perspective on what is. Here are tools to help you find your own way through whatever you face. You will build resilience and give your intuitive self a chance to weigh in on problem-solving. You will have fun. You will find your creative voice and cultivate creativity in others, which leads to genuine connection. And you will feel better.

You may be saying at this point, "If this is a handbook for using handwork for Mind-Body Connection, are there going to be project instructions?" Yes. I will share some of my favorite patterns and techniques, plus suggestions for organizing a personal Go bag for handwork, planning bigger projects and working with others. There are stories of handwork made in and for healthcare settings and illustrations of my own work and that of friends and students.

Two paths of learning are presented in this book. One is the maker's path, about materials and patterns and developing manual skills. There are examples from the quilting and fiber artist realm, because that is my wheelhouse. There are lots of options; after all, humans are makers by nature. Please feel free to use the hands-on skills that you already have which bring you joy. **What** you make is less important than using your hands to **make something**.

The other path we will explore is how to use handwork as a tool for enhancing Mind-Body Connection. We begin with exercises for greater awareness of our whole physical self. A basic tool is to keep a journal of simple sensory experiences. My teachers at the Tai Sophia Institute referred to this as journaling embodied practices. Tools of mindfulness, intention, acceptance, equanimity, balance, gratitude and community will also serve.

As a fiber arts teacher I've been fortunate enough to be a teacher at The John C. Campbell Folk School in Brasstown, NC. The Folk School is a wonderful place dedicated to making things by hand in a wide spectrum of media—fiber, clay, wood, metals, paper, jewelry, plus music and dancing. In their blacksmithing shop, the student's first task is to make their own chisel, the first tool in the toolbox of the trade. Training yourself to pay attention to the daily aspects of your embodied experience is your first tool of hands-on wellness.

As you read, notice the suggested practices at the end of each chapter. They are a progression of awareness exercises which require only basic skills. Accompanying optional project suggestions are based on my time working in hospitals offering creative engagement opportunities to patients, families and staff. Because I am a lifelong maker of things from textiles, the project suggestions will often include quilting, sewing, knitting, etc. Readers who have fiber art in their sinews will understand. If stitching is not a good fit for you, imagine a similar type of project which IS you.

THE 5 SENSES DAILY JOURNAL

There will be a journal exercise to accompany each chapter. Set aside a regular time each day to practice the prompt. Create a little oasis of time—even 5 minutes—when you are in-between. Perhaps with coffee, while waiting to pick someone up, or at the close of the day. Commit to yourself to write daily for 2 weeks. If you miss a day, don't beat yourself up, just pick up again the next day. You are establishing a habit of observation. These prompts are located at the end of the book for ease of reference after the appendix in a section titled Five Senses Journal Prompts.

Materials: All you need is a notebook and a writing implement that feels good in your hand. This exercise is to help you slow down to notice your physical self. The slower pace of writing by hand lets your thoughts and words adjust to a more relaxed pace together.

Each day spend 5 minutes writing by hand what you observe in that moment related to your five senses: touch, taste, smell, hearing, sight. Do this at the same time each day for 2 weeks to establish this habit of taking an awareness break. There will be observation prompts for each chapter.

Be specific about what you observe. Record the facts. Practice reserving judgements or opinions. Omit the backstory. Record just the sensory experiences in that moment.

Finish your entry with a word or phrase of gratitude about the observations you just recorded . Make thankfulness part of your daily practice. Elaborate on gratitude if you wish.

THE 5 SENSES DAILY JOURNAL
PROMPT FOR CHAPTER 1: DESCRIBE YOUR HANDS.

Use your five senses - **touch, sight, taste, smell, hearing.**

For further journaling, see the 5 Senses Journal Prompts section at the end of the book for complete prompts for each chapter.

CHAPTER 2

THE MAGIC OF HANDS

This chapter celebrates our hands as part of our physical experience.

It is easy to take our hands for granted. There they are: amazingly versatile tools right there on the ends of our arms. Whenever and however we want to affect the world around us—to pick something up, move it to another spot, cook or eat, write or type, play music or a game, etc.—our hands are there to make it happen. An injury that restricts the use of a hand, like a cast on a broken arm, takes some creative adaptation to do what we need or want to do.

How many different ways have you used your hands in the past hour?

Our hands can help us communicate with one another. Universal gestures, like hands on a downcast face, can signal one's emotional distress. Jazz hands or applause exhibit celebration and approval. Formal systems of hand movements like American Sign Language can communicate a full range of ideas. Both gestures in dance and signals on the playing field are expressions of ideas and meaning.

The English language includes many idiomatic references to hands. The Latin root word for hand is "*man*" as in manual, manipulate, and manuscript. Our descriptive word, "handsome" is originally from Middle English meaning "Easy to handle, use or manipulate by hand." In the jargon of fibers, the "hand" of a fabric is how it feels to the touch or its texture, flexibility and weight.

We say:

> on hand (have in one's possession),
>
> in hand (control),

by hand (done manually with care),
hand to hand (action in close quarters),
hand to mouth (scarcity),
hold hands (a simple gesture of connection),
give or lend a hand (assist),
give a hand (applause),
deal a hand (in a card game or more broadly, what is given).
sleight of hand (a magic trick),
laying on of hands (for healing or blessing),
take in hand (assume responsibility).

MAGIC

I sit at the arts activity table in the Georgetown Lombardi oncology clinic stitching on an embroidered spiral. A few people are waiting for appointments. With each stitch my right hand carries the needle and thread up in the air and then rejoins the left hand near the table. Up and down, up and down. The hand dance shifts as I make the twirl of a French knot. A man crosses the waiting room and approaches the table. He says, "I've been watching your hands. Are you doing magic over here?" "Why, yes", I answer. "I am doing magic, by creating something beautiful out of almost nothing." The monotonous waiting room has become a place of enchantment and connection because of handwork. Just watching someone use their hands with intention changes the dynamic of the whole room.

HANDS AND MAGIC

Perhaps it is a stretch to call creative stitching a form of magic. And yet, this is an instance when hands move with intention and an enchanting result appears which may be hard to explain.

The word magic harks back to *magi*, ancient sorcerers, and their use of charms or spells combining words and hand gestures to have supernatural power over natural forces. (In today's

Universe of Superheroes perhaps we need a "Threadneedle" character who throws a penetrating line capable of shaping itself into whatever will save the day.) Today the word "magic", as in stage magic, implies a change or transformation which happens before our eyes without our knowing how it is done. This includes sleight of hand - a deft manipulation of cards or other objects, and a surprising result.

THE IMPORTANCE OF USING YOUR HANDS

In their insightful book "The Creativity Cure", Carrie Barron, MD, a psychiatrist, and Alton Barron, MD, an orthopedic surgeon specializing in hands, write about the multi-faceted power of using our hands. Their book is full of whys and hows to have a more balanced life by choosing to include the intentional use of your hands. To quote them - "Remember to Use Your Hands. Hands, hands, hands. So simple, so profound. Whatever you can do that involves steps, constructions, and improvisations with your hands will help you. The hands are the window to the mind, and your rich, creative inner life, which is a great place to hang out. Your inner life is your greatest resource for peace, joy, resilience and creativity. When you make things, you feel good."

Hands in Artwork in Healthcare

My children were young when I began doing creative engagement activities at the NIH Clinical Center and Georgetown Lombardi Arts & Humanities program. Many of their preschool art projects were hand-inspired creations. Wobbly crayon outlines of hands became turkeys with pilgrim hats and wattles. Tny handprint impressions in plaster became tree ornaments, complete with ribbons for hanging. The traces of their hands made the gifts so personal, sweet and meaningful. Inspired by the children's school art projects, I tried using the hand as a decorative element in my quilt-based work with patients. The guidelines for protecting patient privacy prohibit the use of identifiable images of patients or their names in a public way without their permission, according to the Health Insurance Portability and Accountability Act, (HIPAA). And, it turns out that hand images or outlines can represent an individual as both unique and anonymous. A hand motif can suggest traits about a person through slight variations in the size and shape. The series of hand-inspired quilt projects bloomed into artwork for installations and fundraising auctions.

Examples of these hand-based projects include:

Children's hands - The Children's Inn at NIH is a residential facility for families of pediatric patients in clinical trials while on site at the hospital in Bethesda, MD. For many years I designed and made a quilt for the live auction for their annual fundraising gala. Several quilts featured hand motifs based on tracings from the hands of children in residence. This direct connection to the kids which also respected their privacy was very appealing. The quilts were well received and ultimately went to private individuals and corporate collectors.

Cancer patients' hands - With this project for Georgetown Lombardi AHP, I collected handprints from the 5 North infusion patients, who selected the fabric that would represent them. After some magic making in my studio, 3 wall hangings of appliqué circles of these hands graced the walls of that unit and are still part of the hospital art collection.

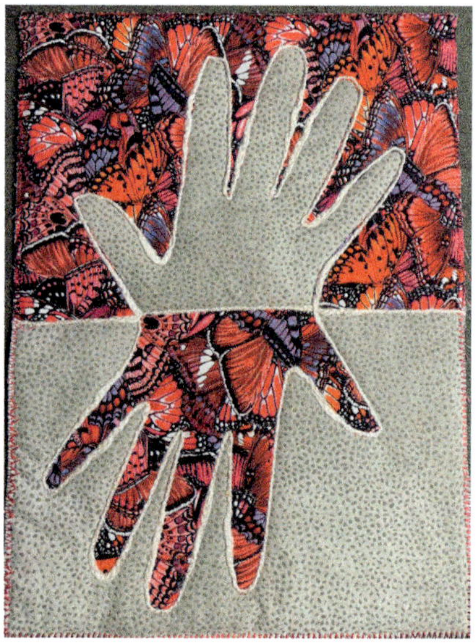

National League of American Pen Women - The Bethesda chapter of NLAPW, of which I was a member, was invited to submit a group artwork to a national exhibit on the theme of "Peace". Our entry featured a central poem by one of our members, surrounded by colorful appliquéd hands of each member. Each individual chose their own fabric print to represent her interests. This piece toured the USA for a year as part of the NLAPW exhibit. It is now part of the permanent art collection at IONA Senior Services, Iona.org in Washington D.C.

Tips for Making Appliquéd Hands

It is challenging to appliqué all those fingers accurately onto a quilt. The use of WonderUnder,a fusible webbing product, makes high quality rendering of hands feasible by pressing them in place and then machine stitching the edges. My advice if you wish to incorporate hand images into your quilts is to practice various techniques beforehand. Photo transfer and printmaking techniques may also serve.

Collecting Hand Outlines

I tried several strategies for tracing hand prints for fused appliqué from participants.

Use plain 8 1/2 x 11" printer paper and a pencil. Have the participant draw around their hand. This usually gives you a drawing of their non-dominant hand. OR a helper could do the tracing, which is better if the participant is a child or would rather not do it. A helper would also make it easier to get a dominant hand if that is important. The drawing must then be transferred to the paper side of the WonderUnder somehow. This plain paper strategy is the least complicated in terms of collecting the hands.

Trace the participant's hand directly onto the paper side of an 8" square of WonderUnder. Iron the fusible side onto the wrong side of the desired fabric. Cut out the hand, remove the paper backing, and place appliqué onto the quilt.

Fuse 8" squares of WonderUnder onto the wrong sides of desired fabrics. Trace the hands onto the paper backing on the fabric. Cut out hands and appliqué. This strategy allows the participant to easily select their fabric. Advance prep is required to cut squares of WonderUnder.

Hands can be photographed and printed directly onto cloth printer sheets (a paper-backed plain fabric made to go through an inkjet printer). The printer sheet paper backing is removed, a piece of WonderUnder fused to the wrong side of the picture and then cut out. Note that cloth printer sheets are more costly than an equal amount of quilting fabric.

General note: *Pay attention to the reversal of the shape that happens when using a fusible. A tracing of a right hand will look like a left hand when done in fusible appliqué.*

THE HANDWORK PROJECT AS A METAPHOR FOR LIFE

The goal of my writing is to encourage readers to use hand work as a tool for self-care, mindfulness and connection. The arc of this book has been reshaped several times, because it was not falling into place with clarity. I rewrote and revised several times, which I have come to recognize as a natural course for an artistic endeavor. No matter what the medium, every project goes through struggle, re-evaluation and revision.

During the process of writing this book I had a conversation with my friend Anne, who is a hero knitter, about starting this manuscript over again, for the third time. Wisely, she said, "I recognize this pattern. It is like knitting with a gorgeous yarn, getting to the second sleeve of the sweater and realizing that the pattern is not working right. If I complete the sweater from this point, it will be unwearable and never used. In order to use the amazing yarn successfully, I need to unravel the whole thing, chalk the hours already spent knitting up to learning, and reknit the sweater with my new understanding." It is my sincere belief that this writing will serve all of us better through this learning experience.

THE 5 SENSES DAILY JOURNAL PROMPT FOR CHAPTER 2: SKILLS IN HAND

List 5 things you are skillful at doing with your hands.

CHAPTER 3

"QUILTING IS MY THERAPY": USING YOUR HANDS FOR SELF-CARE & INSIGHT

In this chapter you will learn how to use hand work as a mindfulness practice.

This book shares stories of how my community of patients, clients, students, family and friends, and I myself, care for our mental health by working with our hands. Our tools have been quilting, piecing, sewing, knitting, crochet, embroidery as well as many other forms of "handiwork". The common theme or thread, so to speak, was making something beautiful by hand and providing balance to our lives. The end product, whether a simple knitted scarf or an award-winning quilt, is only the **tangible result.** The mental health transformation comes from within through the **intention to create beauty and order.**

A basic awareness or **mindfulness** while working on a project allows a shift toward **balance, healing, perspective and understanding** by distracting and slowing down a busy, ruminating mind. The beneficial effects of this slowing down are both immediate during one work session and long term as the repeated task brings us again and again to a more and more familiar place of **focus and flow.**

So, how do we get from "keep your hands busy and do this task" to using your hands as tools for mental health and creative coping? Through practice and observation I have identified the steps to take to make this shift for yourself. You can shift from a superficial activity, which has its own value, to a creative crafting tool for access to a source of insight, understanding and peace. Here's how:

HOW TO UPGRADE YOUR TYPICAL HANDWORK TO MINDFUL HANDWORK

Begin your creative handwork time with a physical pause. Describe to yourself silently what is about to happen; your **intention**. Say, for example:

> *"I am here right now (in this place). This is my workspace, these are the tools and materials I will use. My **goal** is to use the hand movements specific to this craft (embroidery, knitting, origami, etc.) to create something new. I receive the benefits of the **magic of my hands** throughout my mind and the rest of my body. I **embrace the unexpected result** that may show up in the **process**. Success is measured as progress toward mastery of the medium and the **enjoyment** of each moment and movement."*

In Thich Nhat Hanh's book Peace Is Every Step , the wonder of doing handy, ordinary things like washing dishes or peeling an orange become the subject of short essays. They are models for seeing daily life through the lens of mindfulness. I highly recommend this reference as a way to describe ordinary life in a more mindful way. He sums up the daily practices in this way,

"We have walked together in mindfulness, learning how to breathe and smile in full awareness, at home, at work, and throughout the day. We have discussed eating mindfully, washing the dishes, driving, answering the phone, and even cutting the grass with a scythe. Mindfulness is the foundation of a happy life."

As you use your hands with intention, notice the sensory experiences that show up. Feel the textures and see the colors of materials. Be aware of the surfaces and weights of tools. What sounds are made during this work? Are there scents or flavors? Record it all in your 5 senses observation journal entry. Your awareness will increase with each day of practice.

HANDWORK HELPS YOU NAVIGATE THE UNEXPECTED

As a young adult I had goals and dreams of an advanced degree or two, a good job with a future, a life-long partner, a great house, children, family connections. I expected to achieve a plateau of excellence where I could then live happily ever after. That was the plan. Then life actually happened, full of unexpected twists and turns. Within a very few years, my dad died unexpectedly, 2 babies came along, I had to withdraw from graduate school, and my husband's work moved us 1,000 miles away to start life over again. Instead of my getting to choose, things happened to me, and not according to my wishes or timetable. I felt out of control. So much for the master plan.

In response to change and frustration, I sought out fiberwork projects for comfort, to keep my hands busy and to have something creative to think about that was all my own decision. The new house was drafty, and my infant son stayed asleep only when I held him, because he got cold. I literally knit baby blankets onto him while nursing, thereby making additional use of the necessary quiet lactating time spent sitting with him, cozy on my lap. That knitting saved my sanity.

Life does not go to plan, change is the only constant. As someone wisely said, "That which does not change is not alive." Change is the shift from how things were to how things are today. It will happen over and over. In your hands is a powerful coping tool to wield during a transition. Take care of yourself by embracing a handwork project. Use the quiet oasis of making to assess losses and opportunities of the moment. A lapful of knitting is a "don't bother me" signal to others that you are busy—and you are. Not only are your hands moving and part of your consciousness is keeping track of the pattern, but your right brain is also tapping into your reservoirs of insight and peacefulness.

Psychologists call this Body Intelligence—recognizing body sensations as a way to improve our health. A recent PositivePsychology.com article on body-mind integration and attention training tells us, "*To understand our own emotional lives and those of the people around us, we need a deeper awareness, achieved through the practice of mindfulness and the development of body intelligence. Take a moment to acknowledge how you physically feel right now, as well as your next emotional flood of joy, sorrow, and calm. Over time, this can help you feel more in touch with these aspects of existence, and provide you with a rich understanding of your whole mind and body connection.*"[2]

---

[2] https://positivepsychology.com/body-mind-integration-attention-training/#:~:text=Practices%20such%20as%20progressive%20muscle,body%20integration%20technique

As a longtime maker, and teacher of mindfulness and handwork, I have seen that the Mind-Body Connection works both ways. Engaged hands calm a racing mind which leads to greater focus of our attention on the creative task in hand. An aroused emotional state can be quieted through this process. The whole self seems to be more unified and we feel peaceful. Simply put, there are two sides of our brain; the left brain for logic, numbers and naming, putting things in order, perfectionism, and timekeeping. The right-brain is about shapes and patterns, intuition, the eternal NOW, connections. The left brain tends to be dominant in many people but both aspects of our thinking process are needed and useful. Accessing awareness of the right brain and deliberately shifting between right-brain-left-brain states becomes easier with practice.

For a more detailed discussion of learning to access both parts of our brains I recommend reading the work of artist Betty Edwards, author of the game changing book, "Drawing On the Right Side of the Brain." Her training is re-learning to draw accurately what is in front of us, by changing our way of seeing. What we learn about accessing the "right brain" to free ourselves to draw what we really see applies to other creative activities. In a right brain state we set aside perfectionism and self criticism to "get into " the project.

My friend Lucy calls her left brain Nigel. When she is caught in a downward spiral of self doubt and worry, she invites Nigel to go read the paper. She is then free to trust her intuition and consider other options. Nigel is a busy, bossy guy. In a creative task like knitting, which includes keeping track of rows, Nigel has a little counting job to keep him occupied while the right brain makes patterns, chooses colors, and enjoys flights of fancy.

Here again are the steps to foster deeper Mind-Body Connection through creative making. This is a template for any medium and any final product.

How to Set up a Project as a Mind-Body Connection Tool-

1) **The choice to make/do the creative activity - INTENTION**

2) **Giving it one's full attention - MINDFULNESS**

3) **Involving the body, especially the hands - PHYSICALITY**

The results can be observed as:

4) **Allowing concerns to take a back seat - LETTING GO - OPENNESS**

5) **Steps 1-4 often lead to a heightened state of focus known as FLOW**[3]

6) **Increased sense of PERSPECTIVE**

7) **SATISFACTION and GRATITUDE.**

BEGIN YOUR HANDWORK SESSION WITH A RITUAL

Collect the tools and materials you will be using for a project into a special container. For example, I have a box that looks like an old leather bound book to hold needles, thread, a thimble, a threader, pins, and a small pair of scissors. It sits on a side table in the living room near a comfy chair. When it is time to do some hand work like finishing a binding, the box is right there with everything I need. My time for sewing meditation begins with the opening of the box. This act defines the time and workspace as "set apart". I focus on the movement of my hands as they accomplish a beautiful and useful task. When the work on the binding stops, everything goes back in the box, and it returns to its place on the table. The task is completed for now and I can move on to other things.

For an even more deliberate beginning and ending ritual, add an intentional grounding moment of "breathe-in, breathe-out" when the box is opened and closed. You may choose to affirm your

---

[3] The term "Flow" as used here was named by the psychologist Mihály Csíkszentmihályi in 1970. It is described in Wikipedia as the mental state in which a person performing some activity is fully immersed in a feeling of energized focus, full involvement, and enjoyment in the process of the activity. In essence, flow is characterized by the complete absorption in what one does, and a resulting transformation in one's sense of time.[1] Flow is the melting together of action and consciousness; the state of finding a balance between a skill and how challenging that task is. It requires a high level of concentration. Flow is used as a coping skill for stress and anxiety when productively pursuing a form of leisure that matches one's skill set.

intention aloud. "I sit to sew and allow my mind to be at peace and my hands to dance." "This task has brought me quiet awareness of my Mind-Body Connection." "Working together, my hands and breath and creative vision allow me to be joyful as I create something of beauty." Create a statement that is meaningful for you.

As you work, your mind may wander. Let it.

Once your hands are moving in a familiar rhythm, muscle memory will take over. Your full attention will not be needed to manage the stitching and yet you are still sitting there occupied with the task. You are committed to this work at this time, and there is nowhere else to go and nothing else to do. You are busy. Those around you can tell you are busy and will hopefully respect that. This leaves your mind free to follow trains of thought longer and farther. The pace of your thinking will sync up with the steady regular movement of your hands, slowing it down until you are in harmony with yourself.

WHAT DO I THINK ABOUT?

Sometimes it is helpful to be deliberate about the direction of your wandering mind. Gratitude is a good place to start. My mother kept a sign on her refrigerator which read, "Form good habits. They are as hard to break as bad ones." Get in the habit of using handiwork time to count your blessings.

WHICH WOLF DO I FEED?

There is a story of a young person who asks an elder how to manage inner conflict and uncertainty. "How do I know what is the right thing to do?" The elder replies, "Within you there are two dogs. One is a powerful, wild beast, vicious and capable of lashing out in anger to harm everyone around it. The other is strong, loyal and faithful which offers protection and unconditional love. You must choose between them." The youth asks, "How can I know which one will be stronger?" The answer is, "The one you feed." In other words, make the choice to think about what feeds the positive side of yourself while you are stitching.

As you cultivate self-expression and self-discovery through handwork, the distinction between process and product needs to be clear. Using intentional handwork for mindfulness and Mind-Body Connection is a PROCESS activity. The benefit is in the doing, in the hundreds of tiny motions and the mental shift into the "right brain" flow state. The "perfect" end result is not the destination. This is a journey. The project will have a beginning phase and a doing phase. There may or may not be a specific PRODUCT in mind. What you are doing or making is less important than doing something. Just as finger exercises train muscle sets to play the piano skillfully, the scales are not the end result - physical muscle memory is the goal. In the case of mindful hand-work, the activity is to train the mind and the body to be mutually aware through intentional making. You are sharpening the mindfulness skills of being fully present to your whole physical/ mental self.

Once you can move into a relaxed flow state while your hands move, it may be helpful to have some positive ideas, or thought prompts, to give your mind a nudge in a helpful direction. Therapists and psychologists sometimes refer to the **seven aspects of wellness**. As you work, think about how your hands play a part in these seven aspects of wellness in your life. This list is based on the work of Bill Hettler, MD, a pioneer among American Leaders in the Wellness Movement. (hettler.com)

- Social connections - interactions with family, friends, acquaintances and others
- Environmental - the quality of your living space and the larger world
- Spiritual - the great mysteries, values and a meaningful life
- Intellectual - thinking and learning, curiosity
- Emotional - compassion, resilience, acknowledge and response rather than reaction
- Physical - health, vitality, eating, sleeping, exercise
- Vocational - meaningful work, skills

THREE SIMPLE HANDS-ON ACTIVITIES FOR WELLNESS

Here are instructions for three simple hands-on activities using different materials and techniques at differing degrees of complexity. Use them as seeds of inspiration for your own projects. The easiest is stringing a stretchy **bead bracelet**. An **embroidered and embellished spiral** form becomes a personal fabric labyrinth for following the hero's journey of discovery out and back home again. Only basic hand stitching skills are required. **Freeform crochet vessels** offer the experienced needleworker a safe place for the liberating experience of stepping out of a well-worn rut of doing things the "right" way, i.e. according to someone else's plan.

Each activity is based on something I have used as personal therapy for myself as I process a challenge. These projects have served a dual role for me. At first they provided a time of creative concentration for experimentation and enjoyment of the process. As my hands became more familiar with the process, there was inner space for pondering and contemplation. Second, each project eventually evolved into something to share with patients and students. No longer was the act of stringing beads, stitching or crochet about ME and my concerns. It became about tweaking the process for ease and efficiency of construction in order to make it easy to explain. Selecting tools and materials that were readily available, low cost, and adaptable to substitution became important in the context of budgeting for a shared project.

STRINGING BEADS SAVED MY SANITY

After a long marriage ended, I found myself living alone for the first time in my adult life. Family responsibilities that had routinely taken so much of my time were gone. Social rhythms had changed. I was at loose ends in my "free time". Fortunately, the creative work in my studio and at the hospital provided some continuity and meaning . One evening I wandered into the chain craft store in my neighborhood. A big box of assorted glass beads caught my eye, and I bought them, along with a spool of stretchy string. On closer inspection, they looked like the floor sweepings from a primitive glass bead factory.

Some beads were cracked, chipped or imperfect and others still had plaster cores from the manufacturing process. They were covered with fine plaster dust. What a mess. But washing them revealed a wealth of vivid colors and a variety of shapes and patterns. I spent that evening culling damaged beads and sorting the good ones by color, shape or size into egg cartons. Night after night I practiced stringing bracelets. How big was an average wrist? How many beads were needed for that length? How should the stretchy string be tied off and secured easily?

It was an exercise in using what was at hand to create something beautiful. Design principles I already knew from quiltmaking about repetition, pattern and color transferred to this new medium. These first bracelets were gifted to friends and family. Subsequent boxes of beads became bracelets for sale in a basket in my studio. I wore my own bracelets constantly.

After weeks of my own experiments, the bead project was developed enough to share with the Georgetown Lombardi Arts & Humanities Program community. The project is simple to explain; no prior experience is required. It can be completed in 15 minutes. Cost of materials is low. The beads were cleaned before every hospital visit. White paper plates were provided as a workspace for each participant to keep their chosen beads from getting away as they worked. The materials can be transported to infusion or an inpatient room where the activity can be done successfully in a limited space. Each person's creation is unique. The project supports many of the seven aspects of well-being (social, environmental, spiritual, emotional, intellectual, physical, vocational) depending on the individual.

It was a great success. Best of all, both men and women chose to make bracelets, often as gifts for caregivers or family members. It had been an ongoing challenge to engage men in a hands-on activity in the clinic setting. Many women have experience and skills with handwork, whether sewing, knitting, etc. and are comfortable trying a new activity. This seemed not to be as true among men, for whatever reason. Beading proved to be a very popular activity among patients, caregivers and staff across gender and age lines. A bowl of colorful glass beads was enticing to everyone. Men would sit down to create delicate pink bracelets for their daughters. Carefully selected favorite colors became a gift for their nurse. Staff groups made bracelets during wellness fairs and on retreats. To one large family I was "The Bead Lady" and each new visitor to their patient also came to sit with me to make a bracelet. Inpatients clad in hospital gowns wore their bracelets to reclaim their identity: "I am a creative person, not a diagnosis of disease."

Tips for Presenting This Project to Patients or Residents

Materials and Tools

- Assorted beads with 1/16th to ⅛" holes
- Stretchy nylon cord
- White paper plate
- Scissors
- Metal connector bead with ⅜" hole
- A drop of glue like Fast Grab, or super glue

What follows is an AHP training script for the Beaded Bracelet project.

Artist: *(Wear sample) May I offer you a hands-on project using these beads to create a stretchy bracelet? (Open a box of beads to let them see the choices) May I show you the sample? Would you like to do this? Is there someone you'd like to make something for?*

Here's how to do this - You need about 18 beads and a piece of stretchy cord about 10" long. A white paper plate is a good work surface for collecting the beads you like. The average adult wrist is 7 1/2" to 8" around, which is the rough width of the center of the plate.

Pick the first bead that catches your eye. First choice is usually the right choice.

It will be the centerpiece of your bracelet. Pick two beads to go one on each side of the centerpiece. Continue to make a repeated pattern working out from the center. The repetition may be color or size or shape or any combination of those. Whatever looks right is right. Test the bracelet size on your wrist and adjust the number of beads to fit.

Before tying the ends of the cord together, select and add the connector bead which should have a hole large enough so the knot will slide inside and become invisible.

Use a square knot or both strands looped around and put through the loop. Pull knot inside connector bead and trim ends. A drop of glue may be used to secure the ends.

While working together you may choose to further the conversation about who the bracelet is for, what other hand-work that person does, or other ways they use creative activities to care for themselves. The goal is to remind them in a conversational way that tending their whole self is part of the path of wellness.

ABOVE ALL, LISTEN. The greatest gift you can give is your presence as an active listener to whatever they may choose to say. No comment is unimportant. They are giving you clues about what is going on for them. You do not have to fix anything, just be present and say "I hear you."

WHY A BEADED BRACELET IS A HEALING TOOL

This project provides an embodied experience. In a clinic where the physical interactions can be uncomfortable, it is a joyful change to do something pleasant with your hands. Notice that people want to put their hands down into the beads.

Play is an important form of stress relief and a way back to normal life from illness. Creating patterns of color and shape is a form of play. Attention is focused on an enjoyable activity in this moment and the task "at hand" which can break the cycle of repetitive thought and pain, even if only for a little while.

Fine motor work like bead stringing done on the centerline of the body requires cooperation between the two sides of the brain, which helps bring the whole person back into balance. In the Mind-Body holistic view when any part of the whole person is brought toward balance, the whole is influenced, so a handwork project that concentrates on centering in a small way aids in restoring balance in other systems of the body.

This bracelet project lends itself well to being made as a gift for someone who is caring for the patient or some other important beloved. It can also be symbolic as a souvenir, of whatever may be happening today. Symbolic meaning is in the mind of the maker. Feeling connected to family and the community is an important component of health.

TAKING ANOTHER LOOK: THE EMBROIDERED REFLECTION SPIRAL

This project grew out of a journaling practice I learned at a church women's retreat. We drew a freehand spiral on a page and wrote along the line, beginning at the outer end and following it to the center. That was our chance to complain about something that bothered us. At the center, we turned around to write on the other side of the line, listing the positive aspects of our previous complaints. Writing in and back out on both sides of the line provides a bigger perspective on the issues.

One day shortly after being introduced to this practice, I came home to find a damp cleaning rag on my couch. The cleaners had been there and had overlooked their rag when they tidied up. I was upset. "How inconsiderate not to respect my furniture by leaving a wet cloth on the upholstery. They aren't careful. What else did they mess up? Fuss, fuss, fuss." To calm myself, I drew a spiral in my journal and started to write on the line. By the time I got to the center, I had vented my complaints. On the way back out I wrote, "Nothing is permanently damaged. The couch will dry. I have a couch. I have resources to pay cleaners. My home is safe, clean and beautiful. Get over yourself, Lauren. You are very blessed." My negativity had to be named and unloaded so I could fill that vacuum with positive statements. I shifted from a small petty view to a larger perspective in moments just by following the spiral.

This journaling practice inspired another easy and popular project—the **reflection spiral**—which became a complete kit for AHP clinic patients to use while in the infusion unit or take home to work on later. The kit takes about 2-3 hours to complete. The general process can be adapted to larger sizes and a variety of embellishment techniques depending on the skills of the maker.

Reflection Spirals

Reflection: a mirror image; to think carefully; to bring to light.

This hands-on kit for making a textile collage may be used like a labyrinth. The spiral path in and back out is like the spiritual practice of a contemplative journey.

- Sewing can be therapeutic by soothing and focusing our minds.
- Small hand movements create the connections of thread through cloth.
- The colorful, tactile beauty of the materials can inspire our mind-body-spirit connection.

Tools and Materials:

7" square quilt batting
7" square front fabric
9" square backing fabric
24" thick yarn for the spiral
Sewing thread
Embroidery needle, size 7

General Instructions - Begin by binding the edges of the square. Then sew the yarn in a spiral shape using a couching stitch or whipstitch. Use the spiral as a finger labyrinth for a contemplative break.

Step 1: **Draw** a spiral on the 7" piece of fabric with a pencil or fabric marker.

Step 2: **Finish the edges of the square.**
Put the 7" square right side up on the batting. Place both in the center of the wrong side of the 9" square. The 1" of backing fabric that shows will wrap around to become the edge finish.

Fold the 1" of backing fabric in half twice so there is a ½" fold covering the edge of the 7" square. Use a running stitch to secure the top edge of the fold. Stitch one side all the way across, then fold the corner twice as you start the second side. Repeat.

Step 3: **Sew the yarn in a spiral.** Place one end of the yarn on the spiral in the center of the square. Tuck ½" of the yarn under itself to make a smooth end. Sew the yarn on the spiral a few inches at a time. Stitch through both the fabric and the batting. Finish with ½" tucked under as at the beginning.

Step 4: **Use the spiral to gain a balanced perspective.** Take 3 slow, deep breaths. Set your intention for this practice. Think about something you are facing today. Begin the reflection process by tracing with your finger from the outer edge of the spiral to the center. Pause for a moment or two. Go around the end of the yarn to retrace your way on the other side of the line. As your finger moves along toward the exit, consider opposite aspects of the issue. For example, if you need to complain on the way in, find reasons to be grateful about that on the way out. Fuss and release. For further information about labyrinths, see the link in the bibliography to the documentary "Labyrinth Journeys" by Cintia.

As the old Shaker song Simple Gifts goes "*...to turn, to turn 'twill be our delight, 'til by turning, turning it comes out right.*"

SPIRAL STORY

The 2020 COVID pandemic was a time of rising infection rates and deaths that touched everyone's family, friends, and loved ones. It was like being surrounded by clouds of sadness, fear and helplessness. In person classes were no longer an option, so I offered an on-line Mindful Stitching class through Smithsonian Studio Arts. It was a chance to gather virtually to support one another and stitch out our emotions together. My version of our project was a reflection spiral couched onto a vintage cutwork napkin. One particularly trying night I added a quotation from Psalm 23, "Yeah, though I walk through the valley of the shadow of Death, I will fear no evil..." . Stitching those words was a tangible way to grieve and come back out to eventual solace. My fears, and the hope offered in the rest of the Psalm, became manifest for me in that moment of distress. Nothing had changed around me, but hope buoyed me up to face grim reality.

FINDING WINGS: THE ORIGIN STORY OF THE CROCHETED NEST PROJECT

My sons were in their early twenties. Raising them had been a major focus of my life AND they needed to explore the world, make choices, and accept the ramifications of those choices. The sensible me recognized their growth as age-appropriate behavior and trusted them to find their paths. The "Mom" part of me was bereft. My plans and my sage advice for what they should do next were not their dreams. They needed to fly and my nest felt very empty. It was time for me to concentrate on my own next chapter.

For some reason, I started to crochet rectangles, obsessively. My quilting scrap basket contents were sliced into ¼" strips, tied together, and became rag rugs. Everyone got a scrappy, new bathroom rug.

Eventually flat rectangles became circles and ovals. Viewing an exhibit of small 3-D crocheted figures that looked like artist mannequins inspired me to add another dimension to my rugs. The ovals morphed into the crocheted nests. Three dimensional crochet vessels became the next AHP clinic project for those who knew how to crochet or wanted to learn. The excess emotional energy that had busied my hands took the form of colorful nests as a way for me to manage my transition to life without my sons in the house.

Perhaps you are skillful already at crochet and looking for a project. Rather than make yet another afghan from yarn, try to challenge yourself to use previously mastered skills in a new way by improvising with an unfamiliar material or form. The crocheted nest is both familiar and unusual. The form resembles a hat. It is worked in 2-ply "yarn" of 3/8" strips of cotton fabric scraps tied or spliced end to end, plus a carrying thread of 30 weight crochet cotton or a thin textured yarn. Twisting two different strands together makes a strong, colorful and textured crocheted surface. (Image of blue bowl and orange mini bowl) The knotted ends of the fabric/yarn can be left free to look like little bows that decorate only the interior or exterior of the form, or can be on both sides.

The general method is to begin with a tiny circle chain base. Then crochet in spiral rounds by adding an extra stitch every few stitches to make a circular base. When the base is your desired size, stop the increases and keep working around and around on the same number of stitches until it is as tall as it wants to be. The shape of a freeform bowl is reminiscent of a nest, and may be symbolic of home or family or safety. I find it very comforting to put eggs, either real or made of other materials, into these baskets.

Crocheted Nest or Bowl Project: Intermediate Level

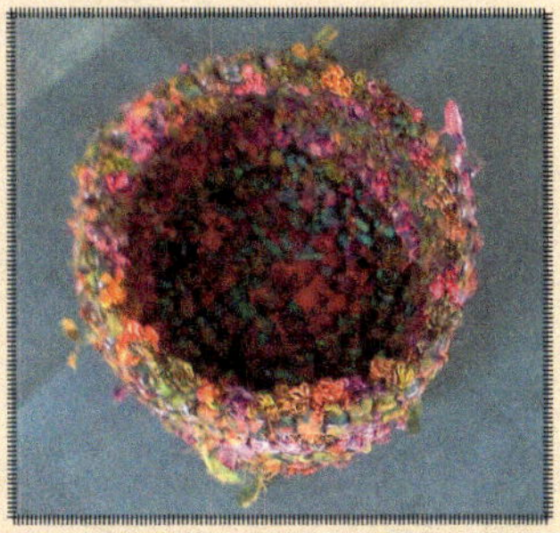

Instructions for Crocheted Bowl or Nest

This amount of material makes a nest about 5" in diameter and 3" high.

You'll need:

- Crochet hook in large size J, K, L, M, N or P, or the right size for your "yarn".
- 1/4 yd. of 44" wide lightweight quilting fabrics, cut into 3/8" strips.
- Carrying strand of colorful crochet cotton 30 wt. or textured yarn like eyelash, in any amount

Step 1: Create your unique 2-ply yarn. Tie the ends of ⅜" strips of fabric together. Colors may vary. The tails of the knots will show as decorative texture. (Alternatively, cut a ½" slit in each end of the strip to insert one strip into the next like a slip knot.) Roll strip yarn into a ball. Hold the carrying strand and the strip yarn together to make crochet stitches from both fabric and fancy thread, a two ply approach, for strength and visual interest. (Two empty tissue cubes make great holders for each of the two yarns to reduce tangles.)

Step 2: Make the base. Chain 5 and work the last stitch through the first to make a ring. Using a single crochet (SC) stitch, work 9 SC around the base ring to cover it. The base is a spiral of SC created by increasing the number of stitches. Work an extra stitch into every other stitch in the previous round. As the base gets larger you may need more space between the extra stitches to make it lie flat. Continue until it is about 5" diameter. (Crochet work can easily be redone if it doesn't look right. Remove the hook and pull gently so the stitches come undone. It is only necessary to take apart the section that is not pleasing you. To begin again, insert the hook in the last loop still connected to the project, and try again.)

Step 3: Form the sides. To form the sides of the bowl, stop making extra increasing stitches. From this point on, work the same number of stitches around, either in SC or in the double crochet (DC) stitch, to create the sides of the nest to 3" or the height you want. (If you want the top edge to curve in slightly, decrease the number of stitches in the next to the last row by skipping every 6th stitch.)

Step 4: Finishing. Work the final round in SC for stability. Pull the thread all the way through the last loop to secure it and weave in the tail end with a tapestry needle or the crochet hook.

Variation - Make your own yarn out of old T-shirt materials by cutting ⅜" strips. First cut off the lower hem and then cut in a spiral around the torso of the shirt starting at the lower edge. Tie pieces together as needed.

Crochet is very forgiving. If in doubt, pull it out and try again.

USING HANDWORK PROJECTS FOR OTHERS

The three projects above are examples of personal handwork therapies that translated into shared activities. These projects may give you some ideas to fold into your own creative mindfulness offerings to share with someone going through a tough time, whether your role is therapist, social worker, caregiver or loving friend. The particular activity is less important than the enjoyment it brings to the other person, and to you.

One of my all-time favorite descriptions of the full experience of making was in the June 16, 2024 New York Times cooking section where author ***Mia Leimkuhler*** *waxes eloquent about her experience making a Fruit Galette. Notice her mindful description of her senses: temperature, texture, color, fragrance, taste. "Making the adaptable recipe truly is a joy. You have chilled, floured dough on your* *hands; a sculptor's satisfaction of rolling the dough lump into a smooth sheet. Preparing the colorful fruit may leave a soft fuchsia blush on your fingertips, an endearing souvenir from assertive plums or melting raspberries. Then out comes the pastry brush—always a small rush of pride to use the specific, dedicated cooking tools—to coat your dough folds in eggy cream, knowing they'll bake into a burnished/wabi-sabi crust. Eating the galette is great too - it is (a recipe from) Melissa Clark, after all... but making it is a wonderful bit of summer arts & crafts,* ***a dose of hands-on happiness."***

COMING UP WITH YOUR OWN INTENTIONAL, MINDFUL, CONTEMPLATIVE HANDWORK PROJECT TO SHARE

A bit of planning at the outset frees you to enjoy the making process. Remember these elements of handwork as a tool for Mind-Body Connection.

- **Try the project yourself first** - As they say at the start of every plane flight, "Put on your own oxygen mask before attempting to help others." Practicing these tasks on your own will give you an embodied understanding of what you may offer to someone else. It will help you connect with the other person on another level. You can create not only a project, but a shared bond.
- **What to do** - What handwork skill do you already have? Do you know a few embroidery stitches? Can you knit? Draw? Cut and paste? Whittle? Make a list of everything you have ever tried to make including non-conventional or obscure crafts. Which was the most FUN? Start there.
- **Logistics** - Put on your PROJECT MANAGER HAT. Where will you work? A home workspace, a waiting room, on the train, at a workplace during a break? Does the project have to be portable? If so, how will it be transported and kept in order while moving? (The chapter about the Go Bag, Chapter 4, has some tips.)
- **Materials & tools** - What materials (yarn, paint, glue) are needed and how much? Make a list of the tools/equipment required (scissors, needles, brushes). Are these things on hand or must they be purchased or found?
- **Relevance** - Why make or do this now? How does this relate to something that is happening around you? My crocheted nests were an outgrowth of how I dealt with changes in my home life due to my children becoming adults. This step is important because it guides the thought process in the mindful contemplation during your handiwork.

KEEP A DIARY OF YOUR MINDFULNESS PROJECTS

Include these factors to give yourself a clear picture of the process, for now and for later on.

- **Intention** - Keep it simple. "I intend to crochet an afghan in red yarn for Nana to be a warm hug when I can't be with her."
- **Description of the project** - Medium/materials, major techniques, inspiration, title, etc.
- **Who is involved?**
    - Past - Who taught you the technique? Who does this project bring to mind?;
    - Present - Who will help or be involved now? Who teaches you?;
    - Future - Who will receive the project?
- **Gratitude** - Have there been contributions either financial or in-kind? Has someone helped arrange for space, contributed materials, helped with organizing?
- **Progress journal** - When did you work? Where? Were there midcourse corrections? What changed and why? Record technical notes, your feelings, experiences during work (conversations, new ideas, insight, related reference articles). Take pictures.
- **Timeline** - Date begun, times worked, date completed.
- **Sketches & instructions** - Keep a record of the planning process. Realize that the end result may differ from the original vision, which often happens. While there may be a set of published instructions, it is often necessary to tweak them to adapt to a particular situation.
- **Sources of materials** - It's important to know where to get additional supplies in case you run out. For example, yarn colors differ slightly between dye lots, so it is useful to keep a record.
- **Where is the piece after completion?** Exhibitions, installations, gifting, etc. Any follow-up notes.

HANDWORK IN ACTION

We have looked at three projects that developed from handwork that influenced my life journey and then became offerings to others. We looked at how you can plan projects to use with and for others. In the following chapter, we will focus on YOU. How can you achieve more intentional harmony among the facets of your whole self through using your hands? I'll show you a great way to achieve this anywhere you go.

THE 5 SENSES DAILY JOURNAL
PROMPT FOR CHAPTER 3: PRACTICE MINDFUL MAKING.

Cultivate mindfulness with a handwork project.

CHAPTER 4

THE CREATIVE GO BAG: MAKING THE MOST OF DOWNTIME

In this chapter we will explore how to design activities for yourself that use your hands to promote your own wellness wherever you are.

You may already have a handwork project in progress which can become a mindfulness tool by applying these ideas. Having a project going in combination with the Daily 5 Senses journal observation exercises and expressions of gratitude will help you become more aware of your own Mind-Body Connection.

EXPECTATIONS OF WELLNESS AND HEALTH

My professional work has involved serving people actively in treatment for various medical diagnoses, or in palliative care in hospitals. Part of my training for this important work was a Masters degree in Applied Healing Arts from the Tai Sophia Institute (TSI), a graduate school for healing arts and sciences. I studied the foundational wisdom traditions behind Five Element acupuncture & herbal medicine and ways to apply those ideas to other modalities.

TSI co-founder Bob Duggan often reminded us that health and illness, or dis-ease, are a continuum, not a two-state switch. His two-fold mantra was, "On any given day everyone has at least 5 symptoms". The most obvious meaning is that every day we receive feedback from our bodies. There are always some parts of us of which we are more aware than others. A sore toe, an allergic sniffle, or a fever—all are the body responding to some stimulus, be it an injury, an external irritant, or an infection. His larger meaning was that we all experience health and body responses/symptoms simultaneously. Believing that "I am the healthy one and they are the sick one" sets up an oppositional separation between individuals. In truth, we are each dancing with daily symptoms of varying degrees of severity. Today someone is suffering and I feel fine. On another day it may be the other way around. As a healing arts practitioner it has been crucial to remember that patients, artists, and caregivers alike are doing the best they can each day while dealing with those five symptoms. We are all on the same side. Start now to learn how to connect and be aware of your whole self by creating an oasis of mindfulness while making something. The hands-on happiness habits and practices you establish now will be in place for you later during tough times.

With all these ideas and tools on hand, this chapter will help you craft a daily practice that will allow you to thrive. The operative word is daily; make it a habit. I highly recommend the little book by Thich Nhat Hanh, "Peace Is Every Step" about celebrating the wonder of a simple flower and the mindfulness practice of doing dishes. Take up his recommended daily practice of seeing the larger picture through the lens of simple activity.

I love the word **quotidian**: occurring every day; commonplace, ordinary. Many of our creative handwork traditions have roots in tasks which were once "women's work", i.e., domestic, ordinary, commonplace. Quotidian often refers to a spiritual practice of simplicity as seen in monastic orders around the world. This book is not an attempt to emphasize a particular religious path; it is rather an encouragement to see more fully what is present and to benefit from the deepening of your understanding through small things. John Sullivan, a philosopher and another one of my Tai Sophia (TSI) teachers, used to say , "**There are many fingers pointing to the Moon. Do not mistake the finger for the Moon**". He meant that the moon represents Enlightenment or Wisdom. The fingers stand in for the teachers, practices and dogmas that guide us on our individual paths, which are not to be confused with the Moon, the goal of understanding. There is a spiritual path that opens before each of us, when we are ready to go there. Seek out the creative practices which serve YOU now, which may include some sacred stitching, or not. John Sullivan's choice of the term "finger" seems especially appropriate in this book exploring the power of using our hands.

A dedicated craft studio is not necessary to practice hands-on creative self-care. With a little advance planning and preparation you can use your hands for mind-body tending wherever you are. Set an **Intention** to work on a hand project while you have to be in a waiting room, sitting with someone else, commuting, or relaxing on the couch after dinner. A portable project will allow you to utilize what mindfulness teacher **Daniel Roquéo** calls these "in-between times" to tend yourself. When and where is there an oasis in your day?

Next, gather the tools and materials into one place to be ready when you are. I call this **Making a Creative Go Bag**. It will enable you to take your project on the road and be engaged wherever you are. In the context of general preparedness, an Emergency Go Bag is to include whatever you need in case of a natural disaster, power outage, etc. A Creative Go Bag is for everything you will need to be comfortable and ready to create by hand, wherever you are. The planning is in the previous chapter. The approach to the assembly of the Creative Go Bag includes elements of:

INTENTION - MINDFULNESS - HANDS-ON - OPENNESS

You will observe the Results of:

FLOW - SATISFACTION - GRATITUDE - PERSPECTIVE

YOU AND THE CREATIVE GO BAG

Down time can be a gift to yourself with the help of your Creative Go Bag. Whether you are waiting for an appointment, during travel, or anywhere, treat that otherwise wasted time as moments set apart for mindfulness. Reading your book club selection or a magazine will help you pass the time. It may or may not contribute to deeper mindfulness of the moment.

The Creative Go Bag will include tools and materials for a project. More guidance about how to select those things is ahead! AND treat the Creative Go Bag as a reminder to be more engaged in your immediate surroundings and experiences by including a few mindfulness tools in your Creative Go Bag as well.

1. **Put down the phone**. *Challenge yourself NOT to rely on apps or scrolling for diversion.*
2. Pack what will help you tend yourself, in mind, in body and in spirit during this precious time set aside for you.
3. Include something you used to love to do that has gone by the wayside.
4. Whatever else you put in your bag, commit yourself to be present fully and peacefully to the experience of waiting.

Creative Go Bag Basics: Here Is What You Need

- **A roomy tote bag** (***Instructions for making your own Go Bag are at the end of this chapter)***
- *Suggestions to tend your physical self*
- **Small water bottle** (lightweight & refillable, to help you pay attention to where it can be refilled and be more aware of your surroundings.)
- **Healthy snack** (fuel for your best self)
- **Hand lotion** (soothing massage for your busy fingers)
- **Personal care items** (tissues, facemask, hand sanitizer, cough drops)

Your Handwork Project

Choose something that is fun for you. Knitting, crochet, piecing, or embroidery may be options for you. When selecting a project ask yourself:

1. Can this be done in my lap? Consider needed workspace.
2. Will carrying this around damage or distort the work?
3. What happens when this work is interrupted mid-stitch?
4. How heavy or bulky is it? How much of the materials must be on hand?
5. Are there little bits that may get lost or be messy?

Make a Kit for Your Activity

1. Use a separate bag for your special project within the Creative Go Bag.
2. Put pre-cut/prepared materials into ziplock bags.
3. Include the instructions or pattern.
4. Include necessary tools like hooks, needles, scissors, marking tools, pins (straight or safety, stitch markers, hoop).

When hands-on activity is not an option, it's important to have back-up mindfulness activities ready to maintain a state of peace in those liminal moments. Here are some ideas of techniques to have prepared:

- **List of ideas for a seated stretch** like shoulder rolls, ankle & wrist flexes, or head rotation.
- **Mindfulness prompts** - For moments when hands-on activity is not an option, try these strategies to exercise your powers of observation.
- **Sensory countdown -** Observe 5 things you see, 4 things you hear, 3 things you touch, 2 things you smell and 1 thing you taste.
- **Breathe consciously** - Be aware of each inhale and exhale. Be present. Breathe in and out for the same number of counts; breathe in for a count of 4 and out for 8.
- **Silently repeat an affirmation** - " I am capable", "I am worthy of love and happiness", "That's one way of looking at it", "I am a beginner", etc.
- **Use a journal/ sketchbook & pen/pencil to -**

  Draw what you see
  List things you are grateful for
  Write about an experience
  Write a poem
  Remember where you left the car.

- **Notecards** for handwritten thank you notes directly related to your gratitude practice.

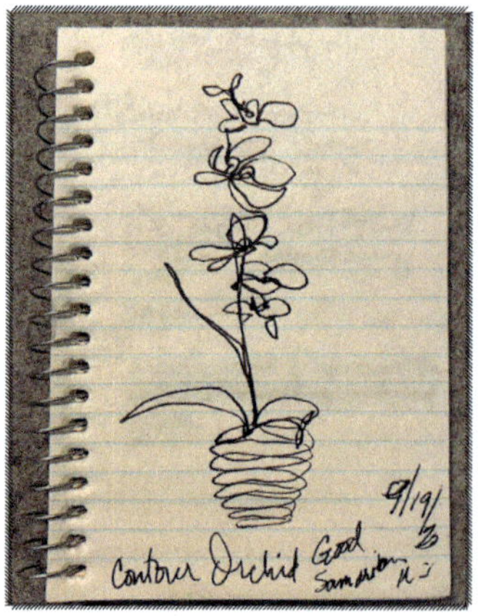

Once again the components of successful mindfulness projects are:

1. CHOOSE make/do the creative activity - INTENTION
2. Give the act of focusing one's full attention - MINDFULNESS
3. Involve the body, especially the hands - PHYSICALITY or Embodied practice
4. Set aside worry and concern - LETTING GO - OPENNESS
5. Enjoy the state of focus known as FLOW
6. Acknowledge GRATITUDE
7. Embrace PERSPECTIVE
8. Relish your SATISFACTION in accomplishment.

Putting together your own Creative Go Bag has been a topic in my free on-line, international weekly class sponsored by AHP about creative mindfulness and movement. Formerly called "In the Studio with Lauren & Carrie" it is now listed on Eventbrite as "Creative Mindfulness" from Lombardi Georgetown Arts and Humanities. [4]

Class attendees at a recent session offered these suggestions to the Creative Go Bag.

- A finger labyrinth
- Playing cards
- Affirmation cards
- Thinking putty
- Bubbles
- Embroidered thank you notes
- Kindness cards to send
- Pocket photo book
- Mandala journal
- Artist Trading Cards
- Zentangles
- Sashiko embroidery

How to Make Your Own Creative Go Bag Basic Canvas Tote

This is a basic lined **17"h x 19"w** tote. Pockets may be added inside or out before the side seam is sewn. Feel free to adjust the size or proportions to suit your own needs.

Materials:

- 18 x 40" canvas or other sturdy fabric
- 17 x 40" lining fabric, lighter weight
- 4 x 30" canvas to be made into 2 straps OR 30" cotton webbing for 2 straps

[4] Registration information is available through the website https://lombardi.georgetown.edu/artsandhumanities/

Equipment & tools needed:

- Sewing machine
- Matching thread
- Scissors
- Iron & ironing board
- Straight pins

Instructions:

Step 1: Right sides together, stitch the 40" edge of the lining to the 40" long side of the canvas. Note: Optional interior pockets may be sewn onto the right side of the lining at this point. Exterior pockets may be added to the right side of the canvas.

Step 2: Fold the lining/canvas piece into a tube, right sides together. Line up the seam so the canvas lines up with the canvas and pin. Stitch a straight seam along the 34" side using a 1/2" seam allowance. Stitch again with a zigzag stitch in the seam allowance to finish the raw edges.

Step 3: Still wrong sides together, stitch a straight stitch across the lower canvas edge of the tube with a 1/2" seam allowance. Zigzag to finish the raw edges.

Step 4: Leaving a space open in the center, stitch across the lining fabric from the corners in toward the center about 4" on each side. Use the opening to turn the bag right side out. Stitch the opening closed by machine. It will be at the bottom of the inside of the bag.

Step 5: The canvas section will be taller than the lining section. Fold the canvas edge about an inch toward the inside so the lining rests on the bottom of the bag. Press the top edge.

Step 6: To make your own straps - use the 4" wide strip of the canvas. Press in half lengthwise to mark the fold. Open the folded piece and then fold again so the raw edges line up with the first centerfold. Press. Fold in half along centerfold so outside folded edges are together as well as the topstitch edges of the resulting 1" strip. OR Cut the webbing into 2 pieces about 14-15"

Step 7: Position the ends of the handles 6" apart and centered on each side of the bag on the inside. The ends of the straps should be 1" down on the canvas inside. Pin and topstitch along the lower edge of the strap and again near the top edge of the tote. Backstitch whenever stitching over webbing.

The tote bag can be further personalized by the addition of buttons, embroidery, stamped or painted designs, purchased trims, or ironed on designs. Make it feel like your own special bag, because it is.

In this chapter we have looked at opportunities for self-care by intentionally using in-between times. It also contains ideas for projects large and small to try. Pick one of these or one of your own for inclusion in your Go Bag. Feel free to pick and choose to personalize the Go Bag for your specific needs. Having your own Creative Go Bag will help you be ready to care for yourself on the road, wherever you may go, even on short notice.

THE 5 SENSES DAILY JOURNAL PROMPT FOR CHAPTER 4: TAKE IT ON THE ROAD.

Record observations about having a prepared Go Bag and doing a creative project away from home.

CHAPTER 5

PLAYING A NEW HAND: USING A HANDS-ON TOOL TO NAVIGATE THE CHANGES OF LIFE

In this chapter we will look at how to manage life transitions using mindful handwork

There is a lot of internal energy generated, and needed, by someone while being in-between due to life changes. Mindful making can channel that energy into the creation of something tangible rather than have it settle into somewhere in the body as stored trauma. It is a productive alternative to pacing or screaming into the night. Here are examples of common transitions and suggestions for relevant projects. Your situation is unique, so feel free to adapt.

RELATIONSHIP CHANGES

Living in relationships is like being in a canoe together. Things are fairly smooth when there is cooperation day-to-day. Conflict is like being in a tippy boat in rough weather, the rapids, or during a external change. There is the danger of capsizing and getting wet when someone gets in, gets out, or stands up and does something unexpected which unbalances the status quo.

A new baby; a family member joining or leaving the household; a new partner; marriage; divorce; death. The choice of hands-on project will vary from situation to situation based on skills, time available, materials, solo or cooperative action, and other factors. In these cases, the type of activity is not important. Doing some small repetitive things that feel useful may be a good strategy to get you over a hump.

HANDS-ON PROJECTS RELATED TO RELATIONSHIP CHANGES

Quilts are particularly common as gifts to one another to mark transitions in relationships. They can symbolize connection, putting pieces together, nurturing, warmth, care during illness. The Native American Sioux have a tradition of giving quilts with a Lone Star pattern to families at funerals to honor the departed. Wedding quilts, baby quilts and t-shirt quilts for graduating teens heading off to college/adult life are common. A cooperative effort among those involved often reinforces social bonds.

Family continuity *- A neighborhood family is in the habit of having each holiday feast guest sign the white linen tablecloth. Signatures are preserved by hand embroidery in the color of the year in between seasons. This keepsake reminds everyone of past meals together and allows newcomers to join the tradition.*

Family conflict *- Hannah adopted a daughter and did her best to love, nurture and support this girl, in childhood and as an adult. The daughter had experienced a lot of trauma before being adopted and carries deep emotional scars into adulthood. After many stormy episodes, the daughter cut off ties with her adopted mother on the eve of becoming a mother herself. Hannah was in the process of making a happy, light-colored, strip-pieced quilt for her first grandchild. When things hit the fan, instead of continuing the project as planned, Hannah took it apart, cut the strip-piecing into triangles, and added black to make blocks. When her anger was vented, she rearranged the blocks again into a more balanced checkerboard of positive and negative spaces with a striped black & white sashing to unify the whole.*

PROFESSIONAL CHANGES

Taking time to process changes in the workplace by making something will slow down the whirl of adapting to a new environment or work culture. It will give you time to think in an intuitive way about new systems and new co-workers. Understanding social patterns can parallel creating physical patterns. For example, working on a knitted or crochet afghan every evening for 15 minutes is an opportunity to sit and process the events of the day and your insights about it. Memories seem to hook into the work. It is astonishing that recollections of conversations or events happening around you as you work can surface again when looking at the project later.

The classic "A Tale of Two Cities" by Charles Dickens describes the revolutionary character Madame Defarge knitting during trials and secret meetings; taking names, as it were, in yarn and pattern, which are later admitted in court as evidence for treason and execution.

RELOCATING TO A NEW DWELLING OR NEW COMMUNITY

Hands-on projects can be useful to help you settle into a new home. This might include making curtains, hanging a picture wall of loved ones, or recreating a beloved garden. Making your new home look like yours can reinforce existing connections and process the feelings of loss associated with moving.

After living in a community for many years, Marian had to move far away from the dream house she had designed herself, and where she had raised her children and walked daily in the woods. Shortly after she left, that dream house burned down to the ground. Today in the corner of her new dining room there is a dollhouse replica of her former home. She has faithfully recreated the rooms of the dream house in miniature. The floorplan, the staircase and the fireplaces are the same. It is all there - from the chandelier in the dining room to the antique furniture to even the lemon squeezer in the kitchen.

CAREGIVING AND HANDWORK

David cared for his aging mother in her own home. Although a professional practical nurse came in each morning, he was on duty the rest of the time and on call 24-7. During the afternoons while his Mom napped, he went to his jewelry making workshop to string semi-precious beads, create handmade silver findings and mount polished stones in settings. One by one the finished necklaces and rings became gifts for his Mom, who wore them, pored over them in great detail and proudly displayed them to visitors. Each benefited in their own way from the diversion of making something beautiful.

Providing care to someone who is seriously ill or very elderly is of necessity a very hands-on role; personal care, feeding, dressing, etc. For a caregiver who is also a family member or close friend, this can be a challenging time of waiting, processing change, and sitting with the unknown. Hands-on creative activities can transform the in-between times into a self-care oasis to benefit both parties. (See Chapter 4 on preparing a Go bag.)

When on duty at her home as caregiver for my elderly grandmother, I used the time when she was asleep to sketch the views from the windows of her house. Flowers from her garden or wildflowers became tiny bouquets for her daily meal trays. A crochet project of questionable usefulness burned off some of my excess nervous energy as I sat beside her, wondering if I would know what to do if/ when she took a turn for the worse.

If the patient has the skill, interest or capacity, a joint project with each doing a hands-on task might serve. Or simply sharing the ongoing progress of the project can provide a subject of conversation for diversion, variety and stimulation. Both parties, the caregiver and the one receiving care, need a break from focusing only on medical and comfort details.

CAREGIVING AND HAND MASSAGE

A more direct example of using hands in caregiving is to provide the patient with a hand and foot massage for relaxation, to soothe pain and provide comfort. It is worthwhile to point out that the person giving a hand massage also receives the benefits of touch, gentle pressure and connection. While not a handwork project per se in the sense of the rest of the book, simple massage techniques are an excellent supplement to the toolbox of a caregiver.

An Appendix describes Comfort Touch®, a method of providing safe and effective massage developed by Mary Kathleen Rose. Her book Comfort Touch® of the Hands and Feet is an excellent reference.

PROCESSING GRIEF

Accepting a loss takes as much time as it takes. No one can set a schedule for coming to terms with an absence or a passing. Parting with personal belongings that are no longer needed by the loved one can be challenging. Special garments in particular can be hard to relinquish, especially when the smell of the departed lingers in their clothing. Repurposing such clothing into a legacy quilt, filled with memories, is a very meaningful transformation. Turning old clothes into something that can be wrapped around someone like a warm hug is very comforting and healing.

Through more than 15 years of having a public quiltmaking studio I have made dozens of T-shirt quilts for someone going through a loss. Client conversations always included stories of the loved one so the energy of the story could be part of the making. A box of tissues is always at hand for when an emotion arises. One client had me make throw pillows for all the nieces, nephews and grandchildren in the family in honor of her late mother. Another particularly poignant example was a husband, grieving the loss of his still-living wife to dementia. He had her hiking and vacation T-shirts made into a quilt for her in the care home in the hopes that she might remember a glimmer of him and their life together.

A Word of Advice About Making a Garment Memory Project

If you are inclined to tackle a garment based project to help manage your own loss or to support someone else, I advise you to find a partner. You will need someone you trust to be a sounding board, as moral support, and/or for sewing construction consultation. Kleenex is often required for this kind of project. My eyes are moist and my throat is tight even now as I type this and remember the love and loss that I've witnessed through the years. What a gift to the bereaved to be able to do something to help them process what cannot be changed. Grief is another expression of love. My compassion muscles have had many workouts. How about that!

MANAGING ANXIETY

Some anxiety is normal in stressful situations such as public speaking or taking a test. Severe anxiety is an indicator of underlying issues when feelings become excessive, all-consuming, and interfere with daily living. Please seek the help of a mental health professional for dealing with ongoing or chronic anxiety.

If you are anxious from time to time, you may benefit from a meditation practice that uses a focus on the breath or a mantra to help you quiet your mind. Recurring thoughts are noted and then allowed to fade, like the reflection of geese flying over the lake of your peaceful mind. Intrusive thoughts that keep coming back are sometimes called monkey mind. Letting go of them can be a challenge.

A hands-on activity can be a way to rechannel the energy produced by anxiety and worry. The shift begins with intention. Setting aside time to concentrate on making something replaces the flow of negative thoughts and worry with a different flow of ideas. A new pattern of thought based around making something shifts your attention from the worry to the project. This can eventually allow an alternative narrative to develop which may be easier to live with. After all, we all live in the story we believe to be true.

Purposeful hand movement causes a redirection of thought, to focus at first on the next actions or the next creative decisions involved in the making. When the movements are repetitive, after a while the conscious mind does not need to pay quite so much attention to the fingers, as muscle memory takes over. That leaves the conscious mind free to think of other things, and process them slowly or at the pace of the motion of your hands. Thus stitching or knitting, etc. become a time to consider what may be of concern from a different perspective. The rhythm of the hands becomes a soothing guide into a state of Flow in which one is less likely to be ensnared by passing thoughts.

In the response to political upheaval Brenda was worried and anxious about what might happen to her family members. She wanted to hug her adult children and turned the energy of worrying into a project she called a knitted hug. Bright colored yarn was knitted in a simple garter stitch into an 18" wide by 50" long shawl to be wrapped around shoulders or placed on the foot of the bed. The easy pattern on large needles worked up quickly without too much planning. Her hands were busy and her mind diverted.

INTENTION - MINDFULNESS - HANDS-ON - OPENNESS - FLOW - PERSPECTIVE

CHANGE DOES HAPPEN AND OUR FEELINGS RESPOND

We all need to develop and utilize resilience strategies to navigate through new situations. We can strengthen our positive response to what we face by slowing down. Something in our hands to do that stimulates creativity and ultimately a sense of control and accomplishment will help, even if only in one realm of life. As you do the journal exercise for this chapter, call to mind your own times of transition and ways you have chosen to manage them.

This poem offers another perspective to ponder while stitching. Perhaps you grew up like I did, thinking that negative emotions/feelings were "bad" and needed to be pushed aside as unworthy. "Think only happy thoughts", they'd say, and then I'd feel guilty for having the wrong feelings. What a revolutionary concept that "the dark thought, the shame, the malice" might be our teachers. Acceptance of the whole self is profoundly empowering. Like the weather, our emotions are fleeting, both positive and negative. (Think back to our daily five symptoms in Chapter 4. Every day each of us experiences numerous emotions as well.) Our subconscious points to something that has happened around us with an emotional response. By letting a feeling bubble up, acknowledging it and then watching it dissipate on its own, we can be more mindful of our whole selves and thereby lead a more balanced life.

THE GUEST HOUSE by Rumi, translated by Coleman Barks

This being human is a guest house.
Every morning a new arrival.

A joy, a depression, a meanness,
some momentary awareness comes
as an unexpected visitor.

Welcome and entertain them all!
Even if they're a crowd of sorrows,
who violently sweep your house
empty of its furniture,
Still, treat each guest honorably.
He may be clearing you out
for some new delight.

The dark thought, the shame, the malice,
meet them at the door laughing,
and invite them in.

Be grateful for whoever comes,
because each has been sent
as a guide from beyond.

INTENTION - MINDFULNESS - HANDS-ON - OPENNESS - FLOW - PERSPECTIVE

Who will benefit from a hands-on personal therapy activity? You will! Along with:

Caregivers - Professional and unpaid caregivers who give of themselves to tend the physical needs of someone need respite and refreshing. A creative oasis can provide the relief to manage what may seem like an unending slog. This includes parents of young children. (Choose a simple open-ended project like knitting a scarf.) More about the specific tips for Caregivers in later chapters

Youth - Teens and young people have much to process as their understanding of the world widens. Taking time to connect with one's whole self by creative making can help release or redirect the energy of not knowing, of feeling powerless as well as provide a sense of accomplishment and feeling special through making. (Freeform crochet and improvisational mixed media might be good starting places for exploration of uncharted feelings.)

Makers/sewists - Those who are naturally drawn to fiber arts skills (knit, crochet, sew, quilt, tat, embroider, weave, etc.) can enhance their work with the addition of deliberate, thoughtful intention. During time spent doing what they already love, they can tend their mental health by embracing Flow as a place of non-judgemental acceptance. (Practice a less familiar way of working to challenge the brain and allow the development of mastery and satisfaction of accomplishment.)

Contemplatives who are non-makers - Those who are already in practice with meditation, yoga, centering prayer, and sitting in stillness can add purposeful hand movement. Mindful art-making is a bridge between the seen and the unseen world. (See South Indian kolam mindfulness exercises in the Chapter 4 journal section, which may be done as drawings or embroideries.)

Emerging and established artists - The role of the Artist is to shine a light on an aspect of the world for the benefit of all. An embodied awareness of the connection between thought and action is a powerful tool for the artist and for the audience. An aspiring artist can use the manipulation of different materials, such as found fiber quiltmaking, to grapple with serious ideas and incorporate additional layers of meaning. Artists with mastery of a medium can revitalize their established artmaking by shifting focus to the physical sensations of their craft.

THE 5 SENSES DAILY JOURNAL
PROMPT FOR CHAPTER 5: DOCUMENT A LIFE TRANSITION.

Write by hand in your journal a brief account of the circumstances surrounding a major shift in your life.

CHAPTER 6

HANDWORK & MEDICAL CARE: THE ARTIST IN THE HOSPITAL

In this chapter I share experiences of being a creative artist using hand work for mindfulness within a medical setting.

Healing happens within us. When our physical function becomes out of balance or we are injured, our bodies work hard to restore themselves to health and wholeness. We seek outside help to speed up this process. The array of remedies ranges from simple to extreme - chicken soup and ginger tea to stitches, operations, medications or chemotherapy. Relief may be a cool cloth on a hot forehead, a massage or acupuncture. Or setting a bone, surgery or radiation may be indicated. All these treatments affect our physical body. The non-physical parts of us also experience imbalance when we are unwell and need tending as we heal. Our mental health including our emotional self or feelings influences our physical wellbeing. Tending our creative self can help restore balance to our whole self.

It has been my great privilege to serve as a long-time visiting artist with the Arts & Humanities Program (AHP) at Georgetown Lombardi Comprehensive Cancer Center in Washington D.C. Within the hospital setting I have interacted with hundreds of people to provide materials, kits, instruction and support for their hands-on component of a creative response to illness.

According to the AHP website, the program "promotes *cura personalis*, which means *care for the whole person*, for patients, family members, caregivers, medical staff, students, and community members. Through its offerings of music, expressive writing, dance, and visual arts, wellness is significantly promoted throughout the hospital. ... These therapeutic art modalities encourage a creative and constructive response to illness."[5]

In a medical setting there is a necessary emphasis on evidence-based protocols and scientific reasoning behind treatments and interventions. Measuring the direct effectiveness of the presence of the arts and creative engagement activities is a challenge. Anecdotally, we know that our mood improves when we feel satisfaction, joy, a sense of accomplishment. It is difficult, or impossible, to make direct physical measurements of these feelings. How can it be determined how much better we feel because we drew a picture or listened to music playing? Can knitting a scarf influence the knitting of a bone? Current research into these questions often relies on questionnaires about pain levels and anxiety before and after an encounter with art or an artist. The research work is ongoing, promising, and not deeply funded. The reaction among medical professionals to the arts in the hospital ranges from skepticism in some quarters to full support in others. Use of creative expression can be thought of as an element of "holistic health" which extends beyond traditional Western medicine. Mind-Body Connection is a huge topic full of opportunities for discussion. How wonderful to be part of the conversation.

At one point I worked as the only artist in a 14 chair infusion unit, offering a menu of arts-based supportive activities. The staff often asked me to attend to an anxious patient with a song, a hand massage, or guided meditation to lower their blood pressure so that treatment could begin. In this case it was not my sewing kits or knitting needles they needed. The intervention needed was a human one-on-one connection experience with a creative artist. The artist in a healthcare setting has a multi-faceted role as both a creative guide and a healing presence. Those drawn to this work realize quickly that their presence is an important element of the dose of creative action. Remember, the finished product is not the goal, but rather the process of participating in creative activity. A facilitating artist must have already done their own internal work of finding flow through their medium. They need to have discovered their own place inside of peaceful acceptance of what is. The necessary resilience and a reservoir of compassion are emotional muscles which are developed, not innate character traits. Most artists working in healthcare have also been patients themselves or caregivers.

Therapeutic hand massage is an excellent extra tool for any visiting artist. AHP at one point provided training to all the staff artists by licensed massage therapy instructors with instructions about how and when to do hand massage. In most situations it is not a regulated form of touch, so licensing is usually not needed, but check the laws in your state. Hand massage is easy to learn

---

[5] https://lombardi.georgetown.edu/artsandhumanities/

and to give. Your family will love it even if you don't share it with patients. In Appendix 2 there is information about ComfortTouch®, a reputable, trademarked massage method.

Bridging the gap between the mainstream medical profession and therapeutic fiber art through BILATERAL RHYTHMIC PSYCHO-SOCIAL INTERVENTION.

Here is the story of Betsan Corkhill. She has been described as *an expert in the use of therapeutic fiber arts to improve health and wellness and manage illness. In 2005 she founded Stitchlinks, a non-profit global support network for taking advantage of the stress-relieving benefits of crafts. Clinically trained in physiotherapy, Corkhill has conducted extensive research into the benefits of handcrafts and is a pioneer in improving well-being through therapeutic knitting and crochet.* Betsan was trained as a physiotherapist (aka a physical therapist in the US). She visited patients in their homes to design post-operative physical therapy regimens. Most patients did not actually follow the plans, did not make much progress and stayed alone in their houses because of mobility issues. This led to a downward spiral of inactivity, depression and isolation.

In frustration, she left the medical field and took the job she could find - a low level assistant at a publishing house. Her assignment was to answer the letters to the editor of a knitting magazine. She did not know how to knit and it turned out that didn't matter. The letters were not the expected requests for clarification on a pattern but rather a different theme emerged. Time after time the letters were about how "knitting changed my life." Grateful readers wrote how knitting had helped them manage divorce, death, illness, job loss, disability, and disappointment. They gained self-confidence, managed their stress, and found like-minded friends in the community of knitters, through shops and clubs. Betsan compared the results of what her medical training helped her see as two strategies for therapy - personal action and social interaction. Knitting can provide both in a way that individuals find meaningful and satisfying.

It became her life mission to introduce therapeutic knitting to the medical world. The first step was to speak the language of the target audience. The way forward toward having the medical community take the mind-body-handwork connection more seriously was to reframe it in the language of therapy. Knitting was renamed as BILATERAL, two-sided or both hands, RHYTHMIC, in a repeating pattern, PSYCHO-SOCIAL, the mental processes that support connections between the person and his/her social world, INTERVENTION, action taken to improve a situation. Thus described, it became possible to conduct sessions for pain management through the clinics. Her extensive research into the benefits of therapeutic knitting and other hand work has led her to author numerous books and articles on the physical and mental benefits of yarn work. She and her students conduct knitting and crochet sessions as successful pain management therapy through medical institutions. I was fortunate enough to meet her in person when she visited Georgetown AHP in 2015 as a guest speaker, in conjunction with Project KnitWell, a D.C. area non-profit that provides knitting teachers to people in hospitals, care centers and prisons.

I was the first visiting artist for the brand new Arts & Humanities Program at Georgetown University Hospital Lombardi Comprehensive Cancer Center in Washington D.C. My job was to ease suffering and promote wellness with fabric, thread, needles, scissors, beads and buttons. On my first day at Georgetown Hospital my mentor, Helen Orem, co-founder of the AHP program, gave me some gentle advice. "Patients often feel powerless in the presence of the medical system. When someone says, 'No thank you. I do not want to make something', it is not about you, the artist. Instead of a creative diversion, that patient has been given the gift of agency. If they choose to make something, great. If not, they have been given a chance to refuse something in a day of poking, prodding and blood draws." What a win-win!

My first assignment was to teach a quilting class on an infusion unit. Five patient participants returned to the unit on off-treatment days. Four of them were new to quilting and were so proud of their new-found skills and projects. The fifth student was already working on an appliqué story quilt depicting her harrowing escape from the Nazis when she was a child. My own first lesson was not to make assumptions about the skills and goals of the patients. Let them lead in their own creative journey.

Thus began my years-long observation of how doing simple, useful, repetitive tasks by hand can help chase away anxiety, fear, worry, hopelessness, and even pain in a medical setting. Prior to this work I had seen my family and friends take care of their mental health through creative activity - in the garden, taking a walk, playing the piano, embroidering, cooking, painting, or carving. I had tended my own health by sitting down with intentional stitching. Would these hands-on tools for mental health also serve folks dancing with cancer? Would these ordinary activities translate into helpful offerings in a medical setting? Art therapists and recreation therapists use activities as therapeutic interventions. The Arts & Humanities Program (AHP) takes a more informal approach, with no appointments, no treatment plans and no assessments. We show up in the clinic as artists, offer something, which might be refused, sit with the willing person and do something creative together. We listen to patients or family members talk about whatever is on their mind. Our job is to be fully present to them in the moments we share. It turns out that these skills are useful in a myriad of places, not just a medical setting.

The steps through the arc of the creative interaction with a patient or family member:

1. The choice to make/do the creative activity - INTENTION
2. Giving it one's full attention - MINDFULNESS
3. Involving the body, especially the hands - PHYSICALITY or EMBODIED practice
4. Allowing problems to take a back seat - LETTING GO - OPENNESS
5. Steps 1-4 lead to a state of focus, often called FLOW
6. The person feels SATISFACTION at an accomplishment
7. There may be expressions of GRATITUDE
8. A new PERSPECTIVE on the situation may be reached, which may include INSIGHT, ENHANCED CREATIVITY, PEACEFULNESS, BALANCE, CONNECTION WITH OTHERS, CONFIDENCE & HOPE.

Note that steps 4-8 happen within the patient. The facilitating artist sets up the situation as best they can. The patient will respond in their own way. Ideally the interaction will be enjoyable and beneficial to the patient. Other responses are possible including not participating at all, not engaging, being interrupted or distracted. There may be factors present that influence a less-than-successful outcome (medications, pain, anxiety, etc.). There is no failure on either side. Sometimes it is just not the right time.

CREATIVE THOUGHT GUIDES A PHYSICAL PROCESS

This is the nub of active Mind-Body Connection and is present all the time. The mind connects with the world through the action of the body. What goes on in our mind affects what happens in our bodies and vice versa. Here is another example of the mind affecting the body, breaking a cycle of distress, and the power of human connection to provide a new perspective.

A middle aged woman was sitting alone in the lobby outside the clinic, staring out of the window. Another woman was hunched up by herself across the lobby. Neither paid much attention as I set up the project table with bright squares of fabric for the day's activity. The first lady said, "No, thanks" to my invitation to sit with me at the table, but the second lady did come over, hesitantly. As we talked over the table, her curiosity set in and the first lady eventually joined us. Soon the three of us were stitching and chatting about colors and our sewing experiences. My guiding principles of conversation here are 1) not to inquire about someone's medical situation and 2) to listen attentively to whatever they choose to share with me. (My AHP colleagues called me the bartender, the one who will listen non-judgmentally and in confidence.) Getting back to the two ladies stitching together in the clinic lobby. It turned out that they were seeing the same physician. And each was undergoing a diagnostic procedure which involved swallowing a tiny camera. They had several hours to wait in the hospital as the device traveled through their intestinal tract, scanning as it went. Each was anxious about their underlying medical condition, and queasy at the idea of a little robot moving around inside their body. The ladies stitched side by side for quite a while in a relaxed way. They thanked me for the project and my time. Their waiting time had become a creative and social experience.

When we step back to analyze this scene we see the first elements of a hands-on encounter. Each lady chose to do something with their hands (**Intention**). Instead of concentrating on the microdevice on its intestinal journey, they paid attention to other physical sensations, sight, touch, sound (**Mindfulness**). They handled the fabrics and made them into small quilts. (**Hands-On).** Each was willing to share their experience and learn from it **(Openness**).

Resulting benefits were: They became absorbed in the project (**Flow**). They spoke of appreciation for access to high quality, state of the art medical care, even though it was icky to have a robot inside them for a while (**Gratitude**). Each realized that they were not the only ones facing this situation (**Perspective).**

Additional benefits were: They relaxed (**Peacefulness and Balance**), they learned that they were not the "lone stranger on a secret mission" in facing the medical situation ahead (**Insight**). They rediscovered the satisfaction of using their stitching skills (**Enhanced Creativity**). They shifted from sitting alone in a state of upset, to working side by side and experienced a sense of community (**Connection with Others**). They had gained **Confidence** and **Hope**.

INTENTION - MINDFULNESS - EMBODIMENT - OPENNESS - FLOW - PERSPECTIVE

A sewing or handcrafting activity might be labeled "a distraction" in a medical context. It may not be perceived as promoting healing for the patient. Notice the shift in our understanding of the story when we rephrase it as an active exercise in shifting Mind-Body Connection rather than something to keep the patient occupied.

An in-patient in her early twenties had been in hospital for 2 weeks dealing with intractable pain even after multiple medications were tried. At the request of her palliative care physician I went to see her. I gowned up and entered a room filled with medical equipment, and fashion illustrations taped to the walls. Even though she was very ill, it was clear that she loved fabrics and designing clothes. A sewing project was an obvious match for her interests. She showed me her designs and I left a mini-quilt kit for her to work on. Within days, her cycle of pain had broken as she focused on the stitching project. Pain-free, she left the hospital soon afterward. Her physician noted the use of mind-body treatment in the chart and I received a hospital outstanding service award.

Tips for Creating a Project to Be Done in a Medical Facility

Consider the following:

- **Who is participating?** Inpatients, outpatients, infusion/dialysis patients? Their companions also?
- **Is the available work area conducive to this activity?** Knitting can be done in a lap. Other things may require a table.
- **Can the project be made in small units or sections?** Interruptions happen. Consider starting, stopping and restarting the activity and continuity.
- **The project needs to be portable.** Provide a bag big enough for materials, tools and the work-in-progress. Written instructions are very helpful when the instructor is not there.
- **Consider safety of the materials (not sharp, not smelly or messy, non-toxic, sanitizable).** There may be institutional concerns about the hazards of using sewing needles and pins.
- **How long will the patient be in your facility?** Is that enough time to complete the project? Will it be possible for them to take it with them to finish later? Are there printed instructions that can go along with them?

The availability of a complete kit with all materials, instructions and tools in one package is very convenient. The cost of the kit and who is paying for it is a consideration.

More and more healthcare facilities are offering some sort of recreational opportunities. Within that realm, carefully designed handwork projects can be much more than a way to pass the time.

Here is an example of a 6" mini-quilt kit that can be adapted by the individual patient with piecing or embroidery depending on their taste, interest and skills.

THE MINI-QUILT

Basic materials & tools:

- 6" square of fabric for the front/quilt top (May be a 6" pieced block or decorated with embroidery.)
- 6" square of batting
- 8" square of contrasting fabric for the back and binding
- Sewing thread
- Hand needle
- Straight pins or edge clips
- Scissors
- Pencil or fabric marking pencil or washable pen.

Step 1: Stitch a 6" quilt block in the pattern of your choice on the 6" square.

The quilt block is pieced before the batting and edges are finished.

Step 2: Finish the edges of the square.

- Put a 6" square of fabric right side up on a 6" square of batting.
- Place the 8" backing fabric square wrong side up. Center the 6" layers on the 8" square with 1" of backing fabric visible on each side. This makes a sandwich of fabrics right side out with batting in between.
- Fold the 1" margin in half so the raw edges of the back and front pieces touch - ½" fold
- Fold that ½" edge over the 6" fabric/batting square to enclose the outer edge.
- Stitch the folded edge of the backing fabric to the front/batting with a running stitch or a blind appliqué stitch. Sew the first side all the way across, then neatly fold the corner in twice as you start the next side.
- Repeat for the four sides. (See the sample illustrations.)

Surface design such as embroidery is easier to work on after the top/batting/backing sandwich is made and the edges are finished. Instructions are below for how to decorate the 6" square with an embroidered or couched South Indian contemplative design known as *kolam*.

Kolam are a design tradition from a daily practice of women in Tamil Nadu, India in which the pattern is drawn in rice flour at the doorway each morning as a "painted prayer".

Dots are placed in a regular grid. Lines in symmetrical patterns encircle all the dots with no loose ends and no line retracing a path. There may be one continuous line or several closed shapes. The symmetry and continuity symbolize the balance and harmony in the Universe.

Making a *kolam* can be a personal centering practice. Each dot may stand for something true for you this day, perhaps a gratitude or a challenge. Drawing a symmetrical line around the dots can mirror how you will move through your day with grace in the presence of what is true.

As you draw...

Let each dot stand for a concern or something you are grateful for.

The line creates a balanced design with no loose ends and nothing left out.

How to Use Beads/Buttons & Embroidery in a Continuous Line Symmetrical Pattern to Make Your Own *Kolam*

To make a *kolam* mini-quilt you will also need:

- 6" square of fabric for the front/quilt top (May be a 6" pieced block or decorated with embroidery)
- 6" square of batting
- 8" square of contrasting fabric for the back and binding
- The dots: 9 buttons or beads
- The line: Embroidery floss plus optional yarn or embellishment cord
- *Kolam* sample designs with 9 dots

Kolam Sewing Process:

1. Make the dots - 9 buttons in 3 rows of 3.
2. Sew one button in the center.
3. Sew a button halfway to the edge on the four sides of the center. North, South, East, West.
4. Align the four corner buttons with the four centered buttons.

The Lines:

1. Select one of the *kolam* designs.
2. Practice on paper first until you are confident with the pattern.
3. Draw the lines on fabric in heat sensitive marker or light pencil.
4. Begin anywhere. Embroider on the kolam line using 3 strands of floss in a back stitch or a chain stitch. OR Use a couching stitch in 2 strands of floss to secure a yarn onto the line. Overlap the yarn and stitch over both ends to finish.

INTENTION - MINDFULNESS - EMBODIMENT - OPENNESS - FLOW - PERSPECTIVE

Healing happens within us. Something goes out of balance or is injured and our bodies work hard to restore themselves to health and wholeness. We seek outside help to speed up this process. Medicines we may take can range from chicken soup and ginger tea to pills to chemotherapy. We may seek treatment from the wet cloth on the forehead or a massage or acupuncture, to setting a bone, surgery or radiation. These treatments affect our physical body. The other parts of us also need tending to as we heal; our mental health includes our emotional self or how we feel.

THE 5 SENSES DAILY JOURNAL
PROMPT FOR CHAPTER 6: SEE SYMPTOMS AS TEACHERS.

CHAPTER 7

CLASPING HANDS: MAKING WITH AND FOR OTHERS

In this chapter we use our Mind-Body connection and hand work practices in groups or for others.

We've talked about the benefits of Mind-Body Connection, about practices to help raise your awareness of that inner connection. We have talked about the ways that using your hands to make something, with intention, can help you connect to your embodied experiences. These personal benefits are valuable for self-awareness, self-acceptance and self-understanding. We've looked at the Creative Go Bag as a tool for self-care. We've explored how this knowledge can be beneficial for patients in a medical care setting and how to facilitate those projects.

Another aspect of the power of handwork is that it can create a bond of common interest between people. Finding community through handwork can foster an essential sense of belonging, of finding your people. There are numerous forms this feeling of community can take.

A long time cancer survivor, Jon, came to the clinic for annual check-up appointments. Every time Jon showed up he was wearing the same long sleeved t-shirt, clean but well worn. It was covered with the signatures of medical staff who cared for him at every facility and treatment session over his years of dancing with cancer. This was his way of acknowledging and remembering the care he received from each person and the river of humanity that had accompanied him along his journey.

JOIN AN INTEREST GROUP

Seek out others who like to do the same kind of handwork you love to learn from the more experienced and share with the beginners. There are guilds and study groups and classes everywhere for being together to learn from one another and to share ideas and materials. Many of these groups have a charitable service project component. Some of them sponsor exhibitions for members to display their work for a larger audience. Whatever the goal, teamwork, or shared action done together to create something, it establishes the bond of a shared goal and cooperation within the group.

SERVICE PROJECTS: MAKING SOMETHING FOR SOMEONE ELSE

Making things can also be a bridge to connect to meaningful relationships with other people in a variety of ways. Creating something for the benefit of someone else gives us the good feeling of altruism, which comes with generosity of time and effort for the benefit of someone in need. The work becomes more meaningful when done for the sake of someone else. Within the quiltmaking world there are groups all over the country making Quilts of Valor for veterans, and quilts to welcome homeowners to their new Habitat for Humanity homes. Groups make prayer shawls for the sick, caps and booties for preemie babies, and even dog beds for shelters. Doing something for the sake of someone else adds another layer of meaning. The sense of peacefulness and calm that kicks in when you lose yourself in the Flow is enriched by knowing that your time benefits someone else also.

SHARE YOUR WORK

More social groups, like guilds for example, have show & tell or sponsor exhibits. Please do consider sharing your work. So far I have emphasized that handwork done to tap into the Mind-Body Connection is about process, rather than product. AND eventually you will end up with something tangible that you have made, be it a quilt, embroidery, a book of drawings, etc. Please be willing to share your masterpiece, made by your whole YOU. Any imperfections or unexpected results are proof that you are in practice, trying and learning. Each creation reflects the time and place it was made, the materials available, and how you were feeling on that day. It is unique and beautiful and it deserves to be seen because it is yours. Your creation is a message about the importance of connecting with our whole selves by taking the time to make something. We can spread the truth that the world of screens in our heads is not where we live. We are body and mind, connected and each caring for the other. Let's be proud of the tangible and show our respect for our handwork.

THE LABYRINTH AND THE PRAYER FLAG PROJECT

We painted a labyrinth on a large, paved and covered area near the Medical School and the hospital surgery waiting rooms at Georgetown Hospital. We wanted to call attention to the presence of the labyrinth and change the traffic pattern from a pedestrian through way to a place for contemplative walking. Through the AHP Prayer Flag project we asked the hospital community to write or draw positive thoughts or prayers on colorful cloth squares. The flags were hung on strings around the entire perimeter of the labyrinth, visible but high enough to walk under. They flapped in the breeze, caught the attention of passersby and created the sense of a space apart. Several hundred patients, staff and visitors contributed their heartfelt wishes on fabric over the period of a year.

BTW: *Fabric squares backed temporarily with freezer paper made writing on the cloth with markers much easier. This very simple hands-on activity was shared by many people in a way that did not require a lot of time or special skills.*

This project had the elements of ***intention, mindfulness, hands-on, openness/acceptance*** *and we did see the results of* ***flow while working, gratitude, raised awareness, and satisfaction****. (This labyrinth Prayer Flag project can be seen in a lovely documentary by Cintia Cabib called "Labyrinth Journeys".)*

COMMEMORATION

Gather friends, family or community members to plan and create something in honor of a person, event or cause. Although a thorough treatment of the topic is beyond the scope of this book, it is worth mentioning here. There are times when whole communities need to tap into our whole self connection for healing and balance. For inspiration I recommend the beautiful and touching book, "Healing Quilts" by Marsha MacDowell, Clare Luz, and Beth Donaldson. It illustrates and documents more than 100 personal and group quilts created with a connection to healing, coping with illness, and the impact of quilts in the healthcare environment. These projects are not uncommon. You may have seen portions of the AIDS quilt or quilted remembrances of victims of racial violence. At times of community distress or loss, a commemorative project is something to do to manage the unmanageable. Look around you for examples in your own community of what has been done before. The elements of building a successful mindful handwork project were part of their creation.

To begin the plan of your own commemorative project, refer to the end of Chapter 6 to review practical considerations for planning a project that include the elements of **intention, mindfulness, physicality or embodied practice, openness, flow, gratitude, balance & perspective**.

THE 5 SENSES DAILY JOURNAL PROMPT FOR CHAPTER 7: CREATE WITH AND FOR OTHERS.

CHAPTER 8

FINDING YOUR OWN HANDS-ON HAPPINESS

In this chapter we zoom in on finding the best self-care projects for YOU.

When your hands cooperate across the centerline of your body, your busy mind slows down. The right hand plus the left hand offer a brain-based, balanced sense of ease. The whole body also calms down, breathing becomes more regular, blood pressure lowers, and anxiety is reduced. A sense of perspective may shift. Peacefulness and acceptance are easier. The mind and the body work together, naturally. All you have to do is pick up your tools and materials and start.

You may already do this in your own way as a normal physical response to stress. Many people use exercise or walking to cope when they are angry or confused. The Mind-Body Connection is part of how we all are made and how we respond to strong emotions. When we feel ourselves in need of soothing, we can channel this natural inclination toward comforting movement by choosing certain kinds of physical activity to move our unquiet mind to a place of peacefulness. Once calmed we can get to understanding, acceptance, consideration of possible alternatives and thereby relieve our suffering. Keeping our hands busy is a healthy, normal way to channel excess energy.

Physical responses like pacing, rocking, fidgeting, thumb-twiddling also show up naturally in the presence of extreme distress, or illness. This book is not a platform to address physical manifestations of autism, emotional disorders, or other serious conditions in our fellow humans. Do seek the care of trained professionals in the presence of emotional extremes. (They may prescribe taking up knitting as part of the therapy.)

LITTLE THINGS DONE WITH GREAT CARE

Discerning and acknowledging personal innate gifts was an important part of my studies in the Applied Healing Arts program at the Tai Sophia Institute. Through reflection, writing, and group activities we each came to understand and articulate what unique qualities we had been given. Each of us crafted a personal statement, or promise, as a reminder to live every day as our essential selves, wherever we went, whatever we had been given to do that day. One classmate, Joe, was a successful day trader—brilliant, highly analytical and introverted. His promise was, "Little things done with great care." Toward the end of our studies he was invited to present a talk on meditation and mindfulness to a group of autistic adults. Later he reported to us, "I looked around the room, and suddenly realized they were all like me, and I was like them." His ability to focus on detail was part of his gifts and promise, "Little things done with great care."

I mention Joe's promise as a way to say that we each have been born with personality traits and talents. Naming and claiming our own gifts has a positive impact on how we use them to make our own corner of the world a little bit better. My own promise is to show up as "beautiful, inspired, embrace", which means to celebrate beauty, be rooted in meaningful ideas, and be sure everyone is valued. (It particularly bothers me when someone is left out in a social setting; "embrace" is missing.) Quiltmaking has been an excellent vehicle for expressing this mission statement. Color and pattern make an ordinary blanket more attractive. Quilts are symbols of love, home, connection, and putting the pieces together; being wrapped in a quilt is like getting a warm hug. Beautiful, inspired, embrace.

As you sit mindfully, with your hands busy, let your thoughts dwell on what matters most to you. What bothers you when it is not present? What are your gifts? How can those gifts serve others? Write about your gifts in your journal. What is your version of "Little things done with great love"?

Make & Take Hearts

This was a favorite hands-on activity at the Georgetown Hospital new nurses orientation day.

It provided a creative break between learning about rounding, charting and how to care for bed-sores. These little quilted hearts are a quick and easy dose of hands-on happiness.

Materials needed:

- 2 - 3" squares of tightly woven fabric
- 1 - 2 1/2" square of quilt batting or fleece
- Embroidery floss
- Embroidery needle
- Scissors
- Sewing thread
- A straight pin

Optional:

- Sew-on pin back
- 6" narrow ribbon
- Beads or buttons

Instructions:

1. Cut a Valentine's heart from the batting.
2. Use the batting as a pattern to cut out a fabric heart 1/4" larger than the batting heart.
3. Pin the two hearts (fabric & batting) on the remaining fabric square, pretty sides out.
4. Stitch around the fabric heart 1/4" in from the edge with floss, through all three layers.
5. Trim away the back fabric even with the heart.
6. Sew on the pin-back with sewing thread, OR attach a ribbon loop to hang it up.
7. Decorate with beads, buttons or embroidery as desired.

This heart can serve as a reminder that you are lovable and loved. Keep this one for yourself or give it away, with love.

The seeds of this book were planted years ago. I traveled alone to another city to be with my husband who had fallen seriously ill while on a trip. There were long days of waiting in the hospital, worrying about him, and putting on a brave, supportive face for his sake. My teenage children were at home on their own, relying on the help and support of friends and neighbors. How could I keep my sanity and equilibrium? Could I, as they say on every airplane flight, "Put on my own oxygen mask first, so that I could then help others"?

At the airport I picked up the book "Don't Sweat the Small Stuff... and it's all small stuff" by Richard Carlson, Ph.D. The short chapters of gentle insights about Life were immensely comforting and helpful. To keep my hands busy, the nearest quilt shop supplied materials for a hand piecing project.

Two blank journals went in my tote bag with the sewing project. One was for relevant medical notes. The other was for personal scribblings of random thoughts, contour drawings of cups on bed trays, and sketches of the skyline outside the hospital window.

Possibilities for new ways to use shapes in art pieces emerged, later to be incorporated into quilts.

Daily walks in the neighborhood became a chance to notice the architecture. Soon I was a lunchtime regular at the nice restaurant down the street. Cousins offered me hospitality. I went to a church service. (In hindsight, I was taking care of my whole self—creative, emotional, intellectual, vocational, spiritual, physical, social and environmental.)

These strategies helped me through a difficult time. The lessons from these days inspired projects for patients and families at Medstar Georgetown Lombardi Comprehensive Cancer Center through the Arts & Humanities program there. They served me again when my grandmother, and then my mother, needed my caregiving support in their old age. And these skills serve me still as I adapt to a new city where I live near my extended family for this next chapter of my life.

Keeping it fresh - Familiar strategies and techniques for managing stress may become so ingrained that after a while you quit paying attention. One way to re-energize an oft-used activity is to push yourself toward greater mastery, or give yourself permission to branch out in new ways to express yourself. Being a beginner again is a wonderful way to be mindful and awake. Suddenly you are full of questions, not answers. There are many ways to learn about a new hand work skill.

<u>Seek out a community of makers</u>, in person or on-line, through supply source shops, craft guilds or through social, civic, or church groups. Meeting others with similar interests will give you opportunities to learn from, and teach, one another. Remember, your question is always valid and someone will know why/how. Whatever you have learned will be useful to someone else. By the way, guilds often sponsor exhibitions for members to share their work which serve multiple purposes - mutual inspiration, economic incentives, and the impetus to finish by a deadline.

<u>Read a book.</u> Public libraries and craft stores are full of instruction books.

<u>Go to an original source.</u> A friend or family member may be delighted to pass on a tradition.

<u>Take a class.</u> Local recreation departments and community colleges offer classes in making all sorts of things.

<u>Look on-line.</u> YouTube has hundreds of lessons on anything you can imagine, and then some. On-line craft teachers around the world teach in real time, through recorded workshops, or by classes available at your own pace, either for a fee, membership, or sometimes free.

Life is lived each day, moment to moment. We do our best every minute to respond to what is going on around us. Our best is all we can do, and it is enough. That said, providing ourselves with a creative project during a challenging time provides momentum and hopefully, a sense of direction, satisfaction, gratitude and joy. I urge you to try some of the activities in the book. Even if the skills in this book are new to you, allow yourself to be inspired to try some aspect of the suggestion that makes it authentic for you, the unique, wonderful you. Perhaps you will be reminded of something similar that you attempted long ago. Maybe you don't embroider, but you know something about wood burning or calligraphy. The stitched quilt may not be your thing, but a mosaic or a collage could allow you to gather found materials, thus creating your version of "putting the pieces together". Plant your garden with an eye to color, size and design. Shape and decorate beautiful cookies. Pack your yummy lunch beautifully by using a bento box.

Here is a list of other media to try:

- pottery
- enameling
- drawing
- painting
- calligraphy
- sculpture
- printmaking
- jewelry making
- making paper
- origami
- woodworking

What matters is that you choose to use your hands somehow, and then apply intention, mindfulness, embodied awareness, openness, flow and perspective to whatever you are doing.

THE 5 SENSES DAILY JOURNAL PROMPT FOR CHAPTER 8: NAME AND CLAIM YOUR GIFTS.

CHAPTER 9

HANDWORK AS A WAY OF LIFE

In this chapter we review the basic principles laid out in this book of using your hands to achieve balance and equanimity.

The power of hands. When your hands are occupied with a repetitive task in which they cooperate across the centerline of your body, your busy mind slows down. Your body also calms down, breathing becomes more regular, blood pressure lowers, and anxiety recedes. Your sense of perspective may shift. Peacefulness and acceptance are easier to access. The mind and the body work together already, naturally. During the flow state of creatively engaged hands, you can gain increased body awareness and foster internal cooperation. All you have to do is pick up your project and start.

You probably already do some variation of this. What do you do when something is wrong? Many people choose to walk when they are angry or confused. *When he was upset, a friend used to channel his agitation by straightening all the cans in the pantry so they faced out. This was his way to create order somewhere that he could control.* Mind-Body Connection is how we are made and sometimes gets out of balance. Choosing certain kinds of physical activity can move our unquiet mind to a place of peacefulness and understanding and thereby relieve our suffering. It is the ultimate self-help that flows both ways.

Shift your attention. Focusing on the creative action of your hands can both distract you from awareness of pain elsewhere in the body. For example, childbirth classes often teach the pain management technique of *effleurage* or gentle stroking which is another small motor hand motion. Active hands can also redirect scattered mental distress, especially in tasks like knitting.

To be clear, this is a coping tool which may allow a much-needed break from suffering, not a cure for serious illnesses. The temporary respite achieved by intentional making can reduce fear and tension and allow the gift of rest needed for healing to happen.

Practice, practice, practice. Deliberately reinforce the lessons and examples shared here as you practice using creative hands-on time to achieve a happier, healthier and more balanced life. Be kind, grateful, and quick to lend a hand. Write in your journal, meditate or do yoga, and talk about stories that inspire. Open your mind to words of encouragement, reminders of important life lessons and nifty project ideas. They will come to you when you need them. Use what serves and leave the rest. Think of these self-care suggestions as a buffet that will provide you with quiet understanding today and tomorrow as needed.

Be patient. Throughout this book all hands-on directions are about PROCESS rather than PRODUCT. Challenge yourself to work in a way that gives you a sense of accomplishment. Whatever you do is enough. Do the project as it seems best to you on that day. In most cases the sample illustrations are of my own work, and your completed work is not supposed to look like mine. Your creative vision is valuable.

Be your best cheerleader. Encourage yourself to stretch by adopting mantras like "I am a beginner" and "Perfection is a myth". Be bold and try something that is out of your comfort zone. What is the worst that can happen? You may create a mess - and no one is harmed by that. In the realm of creative handwork, the dire consequences of an unexpected result are minimal. *I have made a lot of potholders through the years from sample quilt blocks that did not turn out like I hoped.* Be patient with yourself as you practice a new technique. Don't give up at the first hurdle. The seam ripper is your friend. Fiber projects can usually be picked out or pulled out and redone. The personal benefits come from doing the work; the end product is the tangible result of your time spent tending your inner self.

Remember these steps for using your hands-on making for a deeper experience.

INTENTION - MINDFULNESS - EMBODIMENT - OPENNESS - FLOW - PERSPECTIVE

Watch for the clues. This hand-mind-body healing connection is happening all around us. Be alert and you will hear so many stories of how handwork is being used for self-care in some form. It may be done for relaxation, for coping, for distraction, for connection, or with deeper intention as a mindfulness practice. The stories are everywhere—news articles, blog posts, comments in a conversation.

Recently a fellow author was describing her book about the challenges of managing end-of-life care for her parents. For her mother one manifestation of dementia was her fixation on mending old socks, which upset her father very much. The author made an impulse purchase of a cross-stitch kit for her mother and helped her get started. Her mother readily adopted this new type of hand sewing which brought her a lot of joy and satisfaction, and was more acceptable to her father than endlessly mending old socks. What an amazing illustration of the impact of making small changes.

Care for yourself and your loved ones. Remember to include handwork in your life as a tool for happiness, satisfaction, health and connection. Be mindful of physical sensations to remind you to pay attention to this moment. Provide creative opportunities for yourself and others through small, daily life tasks. For example, if a garment needs repair, treat the mending not as a chore, but a chance to be creative and think about that garment. Why did you choose to wear this? Who made it originally? Where did it come from? Where has it been?

Make a gift for someone yourself rather than buying. Thinking about someone else while you make something is a chance to think deeply about the relationship between you. It is a very personal way to express your feelings . You will truly be giving of yourself through your time spent making a tangible token of your feelings.

Wishing you much hands-on happiness.

LET'S CONNECT!

Join my email newsletter for listings of my class offerings and speaking schedule and other news.

Please leave me a review of this book on Amazon. Also on Goodreads or other book distribution platforms.

Schedule a speaking engagement, take my classes, or view my videos.

I am available as a speaker to book clubs, quilters guilds and other organizations, in person or on Zoom. Contact admin@laurenkingsland.com

My classes are offered online through Smithsonian Studio Arts and the Lombardi Georgetown Arts & Humanities program. Links are in the newsletter.

Check out videos on my YouTube channel "Design Your Day".

Follow me on Instagram @lauren.kolam

Gift a friend a copy of this book.

Request this book to be included in your local or guild library collection.

Write to me with your story of Mind-Body Connection and healing through handwork. These stories are important and I want to hear yours. Selected stories may be included in the newsletter. Email address lauren@laurenkingsland.com

Most of all, please **share these ideas** with your circle of friends and loved ones. Teach someone to knit (or your special skill) or ask someone to teach you their skill. Encouraging one another builds relationships and communities. Share your gifts - you will feel better and so will those around you.

APPENDIX

If you want to add hand massage to your caring toolbox, I recommend **ComfortTouch® of the Hands and Feet; A Guide for Family Caregivers, by Mary Kathleen Rose** as a guide to basic principles of gentle hand massage.

www.comforttouch.com

This Youtube link is Mary Rose demonstrating hand massage.

https://youtu.be/r3lOHkfOjVA?si=wiwtthqSkgqUEZbs

This Youtube link is Mary Rose demonstrating foot massage.

https://youtu.be/AUQXKa5LMTs?si=ZuICbxRQ5UivRaKU

This set of instructions, inspired by the Comfort Touch© Massage program, was written by massage therapist Jane Walton for a workshop for the Georgetown Lombardi AHP artists in 2018.

SCR-IBE is a reminder of the two aspects of a hand massage: the interaction between the massage giver and receiver, and the touching techniques to use. Remember, this is a quieting and connecting activity.

S - Slow *yourself* down. Breathe first and center yourself before beginning.

C - Comforting touch is offered, rather than trying to "fix" something.

R - Respectful of the whole person and their response. A tender emotional place may be energized through the touch of a hand. Breathe with them if something unexpected comes up. Healing comes through attention to the hurting place.

I - Into the center. Compression is the preferred movement in this case.

B - Broad movements. Equal and even pressure of the whole fingers and palms.

E - Encompassing. Give attention to all parts of the hand.

DOING THE GENTLE HAND MASSAGE

1. Before you begin, prepare yourself with slower breaths and a sense of grounding. Through speaking and making eye contact, invite the other person to allow you gently to massage their hands. You will tend one hand and then the other.
2. Hold the other person's one hand between your two. Press gently for a slow (silent) count of 5. Release.
3. Place 3 drops of massage oil on your hands, rub them together to warm it, and lightly oil to their hand from yours. (We are using jojoba oil.)
4. Turn their hand palm up, cradling it in one of your hands. Use the thumb pad of your palm in a circular path around the base of the fingers, the thumb side, the wrist side and the pinky side. After a whole circuit, press your fingertips gently in the center of their palm for a count of 5.
5. Gently enfold/encompass each finger in turn, pinkie to thumb in the following way: Grasp the whole finger in your fingers and press gently, to the count of 5. Then with your thumb and two fingers compress the top and bottom of their finger from base to nail. Repeat on the sides of their fingers, again base to the nail.
6. Once again, hold the other person's one hand between your two. Press gently for a slow (silent) count of 5. Release.
7. Repeat from step 1 with the other hand.
8. To close, say thank you and good-bye in a way that is natural for you.

Permission for sharing from Mary Kathleen Rose: requested 8/28/24, granted 8/31/24.

THE 5 SENSES DAILY JOURNAL

Writing in a journal gives you a chance to process and record your observations and your insights. Life is not static, but rather a continuous process of balancing and rebalancing. Even the simple act of walking is a sequence of controlled falls that get us to a new place. We go from the familiar to the unknown over and over again. Adapting to change is the constant to be embraced, not feared. Having some skills to help us balance along the way is helpful.

Here are some ideas from my toolbox to yours. Use those that serve you and be inspired to name and claim your own versions. Write for yourself. The process and the record are both important.

The Whole Self is Mind-Body-Spirit. Each aspect is always present. This book concentrates on the Mind-Body Connection in particular. When Mind & Body are more balanced by closer cooperation, your Spirit self will be affected as well. All three interconnections are involved in the CYCLE of hands-on self care. Keep this cycle in mind as you journal.

1. INTENTION **Mind** - *Make a choice to follow this cycle.*
2. MINDFULNESS **Mind + Body** - *Use the physical senses to notice the world around you.*
3. HANDS-ON ACTIVITY **Body** - *Hands cooperate to create something.*
4. OPENNESS **Mind** - *Criticism is set aside. "Embrace the unexpected result."*
5. FLOW STATE **Mind + Body** - *Float in the focus of being absorbed in the activity.*
6. PERSPECTIVE **Mind + Spirit** - *Awareness of new ideas, patterns and possibilities.*

Repeat as desired.

There is a journal exercise to accompany each chapter - Pick a regular time each day to create a little oasis for awareness of living in your body - even 5 minutes. Perhaps with morning coffee, during a break, or at the close of the day. Promise yourself to write by hand each day, for a week, or two, or even a month. If you miss a day, don't beat yourself up. Just pick up again the next day. You are establishing a habit of observation. There will be observation prompts at the end of each chapter to guide you to focus on some aspect of your expanding awareness of how your body responds to an experience.

Materials - All you need is a notebook and a writing tool that feels comfortable in your hand. This exercise is to help you slow down to notice your physical self. The slower pace of writing by hand allows your thoughts and words to adjust to a more relaxed pace together.

The assignment - Each day spend 5 minutes writing by hand what you notice happening *in your body* using one or more of your five senses - touch, taste, smell, hearing, sight. Do this at the same time each day for two weeks to establish this habit of taking a physical awareness break. You may repeat the prompts or skip around to do them in the order that serves you. Prompts 2, 3, 5, and 6 can be modified to focus on different activities or experiences.

Be specific about the physical sensations you observe. Record just the sensory experiences of that moment. Leave out the backstory, judgements or complaints. For example, as I write this I will say, "My fingers are a little cold, my skin feels dry. I hear a swishing sound when I rub my hands together." The phrase "How about that!" sums up an observation without passing judgement or assigning blame. Of course I may choose to act based on these observations, by turning up the heat, applying hand lotion or putting on gloves.

Finish your entry with a word or phrase of gratitude. Make thankfulness part of your daily practice. Elaborate on what you are grateful for if you wish. This will engage your Mind-Body Connection at this moment. For example, "I am grateful to have hands that can do so many things and lotion to keep them in good condition.

THE 5 SENSES DAILY JOURNAL
PROMPT FOR CHAPTER 1: DESCRIBE YOUR HANDS.

Use your five senses - **touch, sight, taste, smell, hearing.**

Touch - Describe the feel of the skin on different parts of your hands. Compare the texture of your forearms, top and bottom, to your palms.

Sight - Write about visual texture and colors on your hands. How are they different in various areas? Describe the nails, or any scars or veins.

Taste - One of our earliest routes to getting to know our hands is through taste - babies love stuffingdf fingers in their mouths. Give yourself permission as an adult once again to explore the taste and feel of your hand this way. What do you observe?

Smell - What fragrances linger on your fingers?

Hearing - What sounds can you create with your hands?

To wrap up, be specific about what you observe. A sentence or two is enough. Record the facts and reserve value judgements or opinions. Omit the backstory. Record just the sensory experiences you notice in this precious moment.

Finish your entry with a word or phrase of **gratitude** about the observations you just recorded. Make thankfulness part of your daily practice.

THE 5 SENSES DAILY JOURNAL PROMPT FOR CHAPTER 2: SKILLS IN HAND

List 5 things you are skillful at doing with your hands. (Feel free to expand this list as you think of more things.)

How did you learn to do each of these 5 things?

Why do you love doing this?

Does doing this influence how the rest of you feels, physically or mentally?

As you do one of these skillful things, record how your five senses are involved.

Touch -

Sight -

Taste -

Smell -

Sound -

Bonus prompt - Make a continuous line pencil drawing of your non-dominant hand without picking up the pencil or looking at the paper. Keep your eyes on the contours of the shapes of your fingers. The goal is slow observation of your hand, not perfection of rendering or drawing. The drawing may look strange, AND you will have seen your own hands in a new way.

INTENTION - MINDFULNESS - EMBODIMENT - OPENNESS - FLOW - PERSPECTIVE

THE 5 SENSES DAILY JOURNAL PROMPT FOR CHAPTER 3: PRACTICE MINDFUL MAKING.

Cultivate mindfulness with a handwork project. Select one of the projects presented in Chapter 3 to follow the steps for mindful making below.

1. **The choice to make/do the creative activity - INTENTION**
2. **Give it one's full attention - MINDFULNESS**
3. **Involve the body, especially the hands - PHYSICALITY**
4. **Allow concerns to take a back seat - LETTING GO - OPENNESS**
5. **Steps 1-4 often lead to a heightened state of focus known as FLOW**
6. **Increased sense of PERSPECTIVE**
7. **SATISFACTION and GRATITUDE.**

As you use your hands, notice with your five senses - Touch, Sight, Taste, Smell, Hearing. Record your observations.

To wrap up, be specific about what you observe. Keep it concise. Record the facts and reserve value judgements or opinions. Be in the moment. All we have is right now. Looking back at past disappointments or failures is useful only as a learning opportunity. Projecting ahead is merely guesswork. Assumptions about the future are not reality, only ideas.

Finish your entry with a word or phrase of gratitude about the observations you just recorded. Make thankfulness part of your daily practice. Elaborate on gratitude if you wish.

Bonus activity - Once you get into a flow state, you may choose to focus on one of the seven aspects of wellness in your own life.

Social - positive relationships with friends, family, and community

Environmental - a safe, comfortable home; concern for the natural world around you

Spiritual - beliefs and values that shape and guide your decisions; a meaningful life

Emotional - resilience, attention to your mind and feelings

Intellectual - curiosity, on-going willingness to learn new skills and ideas

Physical - care and nurture of your body through eating carefully, exercise and sleep

Occupational - your work and your avocations that are fulfilling

What feeds you in each aspect? What needs more tending? Remember, you are already whole, and always capable of growth and change.

INTENTION - MINDFULNESS - EMBODIMENT - OPENNESS - FLOW - PERSPECTIVE

THE 5 SENSES DAILY JOURNAL PROMPT FOR CHAPTER 4: TAKE IT ON THE ROAD.

Record observations about having a prepared Go Bag and doing a creative project away from home.

Customize a small creative Go Bag as described in Chapter 4 for the next time you face 15 minutes of possible wait time. Adjust the contents to that specific place and situation. Waits in a medical office, at a bus stop or in a carpool line in front of a school are different sized workspaces and allow for differing levels of concentration. Take the bag along and try it out.

Observe and record in your journal the results. How did a prepared activity affect your waiting? Was it helpful? Was it a pressure creator rather than a pressure reliever? What could be changed to make it more helpful? *Remember that "failures" are excellent pointers to improvement.* Expect to refine and adapt your Creative Go Bag to changing situations. The goal is to be prepared.

As you use the Go Bag, observe your hands. Pay attention with your five senses. Record what happens, if anything.

Touch -

Sight -

Taste -

Smell -

Sound -

Record your observations in your journal.

To wrap up, be specific about what you observe. Keep it concise. Record the facts and reserve value judgements or opinions.

Finish your entry with a word or phrase of gratitude about the observations you just recorded. Make thankfulness part of your daily practice. Elaborate on gratitude if you wish.

INTENTION - MINDFULNESS - EMBODIMENT - OPENNESS - FLOW - PERSPECTIVE

THE 5 SENSES DAILY JOURNAL
PROMPT FOR CHAPTER 5: DOCUMENT A LIFE TRANSITION.

Write by hand in your journal a brief account of the circumstances surrounding a major shift in your life.

What physical responses did you experience? (Tears, muscle aches, stomach upset, headaches, insomnia)

Did you use physical activity as a way to help you cope? (Walking or exercise, making something, organizing, cleaning, music making)

Which physical tools that you used then were the most useful? Be specific about what you observe/recall.

Record the facts - Practice reserving judgements or opinions. Omit the backstory. Record just the sensory experiences you remember from that experience.

Include all of your five senses - **touch, sight, taste, smell, hearing**.

Touch - Describe what you felt with your hands, and the rest of your body.

Sight - Write about visual textures and colors.

Taste - Did flavors play a part?

Smell - What odors were present?

Hearing - What sounds played a part?

To wrap up, be specific about what you observe. Keep it concise. Record the facts and reserve value judgements or opinions.

Finish your entry with a word or phrase of gratitude about the observations you just recorded. Make thankfulness part of your daily practice. Elaborate on gratitude if you wish.

INTENTION - MINDFULNESS - EMBODIMENT - OPENNESS - FLOW - PERSPECTIVE

THE 5 SENSES DAILY JOURNAL PROMPT FOR CHAPTER 6: SEE SYMPTOMS AS TEACHERS.

(Refer to Chapter 5 for more on this idea.) Every day each of us feels at least 5 symptoms, major or minor. *These are not to be confused with the 5 senses, which are tools we have all the time. The 5 (more or less) symptoms we're talking about here are out-of-the-ordinary sensations from the body which may signal that something is wrong. A runny nose or an aching muscle are examples of symptoms.*

What are your 5 symptoms today? Where do they show up in your body? Describe how your body feels in terms of your 5 senses. This exercise is only about noticing. Diagnosis and treatment are another step.

List at least 5 symptoms you are experiencing today by scanning your 5 senses.

Touch -

Sight -

Taste -

Smell -

Sound -

Record your observations.

To wrap up, be specific about what you observe. Keep it concise. Record the facts and reserve value judgements or opinions.

You may ask, "Why does this 5 symptom exercise follow the chapter about creative activity in the hospital?" It's placed here to reinforce the idea that health and disease are an ever-shifting continuum. Patients and caregivers need to be aware that the caregiver of today could be the patient of tomorrow, and vice versa. Particularly for a "well person" who is considering using their handwork gifts to serve those who are "not well", it is a respectful reminder that we are all equals, experiencing our unique life paths. Each of us is always a whole person. There is no "them" or "us", there is only "all of us".

Finish your journal entry with a word or phrase of gratitude about the observations you just recorded. Make thankfulness part of your daily practice. Elaborate on gratitude if you wish.

INTENTION - MINDFULNESS - EMBODIMENT - OPENNESS - FLOW - PERSPECTIVE

THE 5 SENSES DAILY JOURNAL
PROMPT FOR CHAPTER 7: CREATE WITH AND FOR OTHERS.

Who or what might you want to commemorate with a handwork project? Why is this person or story important to you? What would be an appropriate tribute?

OR Who needs something you can make to ease their load? Why do you care?

Do you feel a physical change when you think about this? If so, this is a Mind-Body Connection observation. Emotional responses often show up as physical sensations. Old emotional memories can trigger physical "symptoms" or responses once again even years later. How about that! These remembered sensations can be just as real later on as they were at the original experience. There is nothing wrong - this is a chance to understand how your past experience can influence how your body is feeling today.

As you ponder creating a commemorative or service handwork project, pay attention to your five senses. Not every sense may be involved; notice what you do feel.

Touch -

Sight -

Taste -

Smell -

Sound -

Bonus Activity - Partnership - Write about someone with whom you are a partner in working toward a common goal. OR Write about a group project that you would like to see become a reality.

INTENTION - MINDFULNESS - EMBODIMENT - OPENNESS - FLOW - PERSPECTIVE

THE 5 SENSES DAILY JOURNAL
PROMPT FOR CHAPTER 8: NAME AND CLAIM YOUR GIFTS.

As you mindfully knit or stitch or do your project of the day, let your thoughts dwell on your gifts and strengths. For example, are you detail oriented or a big picture thinker? Are you inclined toward action or caution? Toward independence or putting others first? The world needs all these things, so whatever you have to offer is valuable. What feedback do you get from others who really know you? How can you use your gifts to serve others?

Start with a list of **three** gifts in your journal and add to that as you go. What is your version of "Little things done with great love"? When you offer your gifts to the world, you are giving of your best self.

My gifts are:

How do I use these gifts to serve others?

Reminders for engaging the Five Senses in light of your gifts and promise.

Touch - Describe what you feel throughout your body.

Sight - What do you see?

Taste - What do you observe in your mouth?

Smell - Are fragrances present?

Hearing - What sounds can you hear?

To wrap up, be specific about what you observe. A sentence or two is enough. Record the facts and reserve value judgements or opinions. Omit the backstory. Record just the sensory experiences you notice in this precious moment.

Finish your entry with a word or phrase of gratitude about the observations you just recorded. Make thankfulness part of your daily practice. Elaborate on gratitude if you wish.

Bonus activity - Tell someone else about a little thing that they do well; their gift. For example, "I admire your attention to details," or "Thank you for your kindness and friendliness to me when I was new." Everyone has been given gifts. Acknowledging them in others helps everyone stand a little taller.

INTENTION - MINDFULNESS - EMBODIMENT - OPENNESS - FLOW - PERSPECTIVE

THE 5 SENSES DAILY JOURNAL
CHOOSE YOUR OWN ADVENTURE

Going forward, use this format to record whatever experience is meaningful or challenging for you.

Record whatever of your five senses may have changed - **touch, sight, taste, smell, hearing**.

Touch - Is there a tightness in your throat or elsewhere?

Sight - Is there a difference in how your eyes feel?

Taste - Is your mouth dry? How is your stomach?

Smell - Are there smells present, if any?

Hearing - What sounds can you hear from nearby? From far away?

To wrap up, be specific about what you observe. A sentence or two is enough. Record the facts and reserve value judgements or opinions. Omit the backstory. Record just the sensory experiences you notice in this precious moment.

Finish your entry with a word or phrase of gratitude about the observations you just recorded. Make thankfulness part of your daily practice. Elaborate on gratitude if you wish.

INTENTION - MINDFULNESS - EMBODIMENT - OPENNESS - FLOW - PERSPECTIVE

BOOKLIST

SUGGESTED READINGS AND AUTHORS-

Barks, Coleman, translator - *The Essential Rumi,* Harper One, 2004

Cabib, Cintia - documentary film, *Labyrinth Journeys,* 2016 *Labyrinth Journeys | Cintia Cabib*

Barron, Carrie M.D. and Barron, Alton M.D. - *The Creativity Cure,* Scribner, 2012

Cameron, Julia - *The Artist's Way,* Tarcher Putnam, 1992

Richard Carlson Ph.D. - *Don't Sweat the Small Stuff...and it's all small stuff,* Hyperion, 1997

Dianne M. Connelly - *Medicine Words,* Tai Sophia Press, 2009

Betsan Corkhill - *Knit for Health and Wellness,* Flatbear Publishing, 2014

Betty Edwards - *Drawing on the Right Side of the Brain,* Tarcher Perigee, 2012

Thich Nhat Hanh, *Peace is Every Step,* Bantam Books, 1991

Lauren Kingsland - *Healing Journey,* CQS Press, 2013

The Extraordinary T-Shirt Quilt, CQS Press, 2006

Thomas Moore - *Care of the Soul,* Harper Collins,1992

The Care of the Soul in Medicine, Hay House, 2010

Kathleen Norris - *The Quotidian Mysteries*, Paulist Press, 1998

Mary Kathleen Rose, *Comfort Touch® of the Hands and Feet*, www.comforttouch.com, 2015

John G. Sullivan - *The Fourfold Path to Wholeness*, Second Journey Publications, 2010

Living Large, Tai Sophia Press, 2004

Integral Living, Second Journey Publications, 2014

Jon Kabat-Zinn - *Wherever You Go There You Are*, Hyperion, 1994

Printed in Great Britain
by Amazon

61902732R00058